History,
Frontier,
and Section

Frederick Jackson Turner in his office
at the Wisconsin Historical Society quarters in the State Capitol.
(Courtesy, State Historical Society of Wisconsin, WHi(X3)35004.)

History, Frontier, and Section

THREE ESSAYS BY
Frederick Jackson Turner

Introduction by Martin Ridge

UNIVERSITY OF NEW MEXICO PRESS
Albuquerque

Library of Congress Cataloging-in-Publication Data

Turner, Frederick Jackson, 1861–1932.
History, frontier, and section: three essays / by Frederick Jackson Turner;
introduction by Martin Ridge.—1st ed.
p.   cm.
Contents: The significance of history (1891)—
The significance of the frontier in American history (1893)—
The significance of the section in American history (1925).
ISBN 0–8263–1426–0.
ISBN 0–8263–1432–5 (pbk.)
1. Frontier thesis. 2. West (U.S.)—History. 3. Sectionalism (United States).
4. United States—History—Philosophy. 5.United States—Territorial
expansion. 6. Frontier and pioneer life—United States.
I. Ridge, Martin. II. Title.
E179.5 T957 1993
973.8—dc20
92-42709
CIP

History, Frontier & Section was designed by Emmy Ezzell,
and typeset by computer, using PageMaker 4.0 software
with Granjon type from the Adobe Type Library.
It was printed and bound by BookCrafters, Inc.,
on acid-free Glatfelter paper.

For historians
who enjoy reading about
how their distinguished predecessors
thought and wrote
about the past.

Contents

Introduction

Martin Ridge

Although a time may come when American historians are no longer interested in the scholarly contributions of Frederick Jackson Turner, that era has not yet arrived. Over the past three quarters of a century his work has received more critical attention than that of any historian since William Bradford.[1] His studies on the role of sections in an understanding of American culture and politics and on the importance of the frontier to American national development still cast a long shadow across several scholarly disciplines.[2] Moreover, many of Turner's ideas—often in a thoroughly diluted fashion—have entered into the mainstream of national popular thought. So remarkable has been the impact of Turner's initial frontier essay on both the academic and lay public that it has been termed a masterpiece.[3] If for no other reason, this justifies the publication of the following three essays, which say much about a master historian and American history.

Yet, almost from the start, criticisms of Turner's work mounted as steadily as his popularity.[4] Many historians of the post–World War II era feel Turner, who did not write many books, was not prolific enough, although he wrote more than a score of articles. In fact, he has been viewed as something of a professional failure, never managing to complete the serious monograph that would have validated his frontier thesis.[5] Critics of his thesis, however, have had a hard time escaping from his paradigm.[6] In an odd turn of

events, current critics of Turner have made his name something
of a household word by attacking his frontier ideas in the pages of
the *New York Times Magazine* (March 18, 1990) and *U.S. News and
World Report* (May 21, 1990), presenting his thought as if he were
alive, rather than deceased for more than half a century. Turner's
views on sectionalism have also achieved something of a life of
their own, having been taken up and modified by geographers,
sociologists, political scientists, and cultural historians.[7]

An understanding of Frederick Jackson Turner's historical
studies is possible only in the context of his life. He always insisted
that his personal experience profoundly influenced his scholarly
thinking. Turner was a college professor. His status in the profession, his role in the university, and the influence of his life on the
evolution of his thought are crucial to understanding his scholarship. His generation of historians accepted evolution, believed in
progress, trusted in democracy, and held that the social and economic problems of a modernizing society could be resolved
through rational means. They were dedicated to science and
sought the professionalization of history as a scholarly discipline
instead of its being the home of an amateur literati. Turner shared
these beliefs.

Turner was born in Portage, Columbia County, Wisconsin on
November 14, 1861.[8] His parents—Andrew Jackson Turner and
Mary Hanford Turner—were of New England stock, a people
who had drifted westward, first to New York and then to the Old
Northwest. Andrew Jackson Turner, who arrived in Portage in
1855, had gone West to grow up with the country. Mary Hanford
Turner, the daughter of a townsite speculator, had taught school
in the new village of Friendship, Wisconsin. As her husband's career advanced from journeyman printer to publisher of a local
newspaper, from state legislator to mayor, and from newcomer to
local railroad promoter, Mary Turner looked after her home.
Frederick Jackson Turner was the first of her several children.

During his boyhood Frederick Jackson Turner learned liberal

Republican politics from his father's table talk and associates. He came to understand the nature of the political process, of ethnic voting blocs, and of the mechanics of party behavior.[9] His father's intermittent financial success also demonstrated the possibilities that existed in nineteenth-century small-town America for a hard-working and ambitious man who was willing to risk and invest his capital. As Turner grew to manhood, he found his place in a family situated in the nation's white, small-town, middle-class elite. Turner received his formal education in the Portage public schools, where he earned a reputation as an outstanding student and stirring orator. He had already read widely, but compared to students who prepared carefully for higher education, Turner was hardly ready for college life. He later reminisced that setting type for the family newspaper proved to be his real education, exposing him to the world of politics and economics.

White men had long been familiar with Portage and its environs by the time of Turner's youth. The town had been on the old fur-trade route south from Green Bay to the Mississippi River; it was a major logging community in the 1870s; and it was an important farm marketing town in the decades after the Civil War. Portage was also a county seat. As a boy Turner enjoyed the world of semirural Wisconsin, especially the fishing, a hobby he pursued during much of his life. Turner liked to remember Portage as something out of Tom Sawyer's America, with Indians, rivermen, loggers, and toughs enriching its history and life. Nevertheless, Portage was an "up-and-coming" town, boasting almost four thousand inhabitants in 1870, but it still bore the scars, lynching for instance, of a frontier village. And given that mid-century Wisconsin was a state of many immigrant groups, Columbia County was home to a diverse population.[10]

Although Turner lacked the best formal education, he carried special cultural baggage when he made the short trip from Portage to the University of Wisconsin at Madison for what was the beginning of a life-long intellectual odyssey. He possessed an

Emersonian appreciation of nature, a pride in national economic development, a belief in the efficacy of democratic growth and change, and a powerful will to succeed. Like many young men of his generation, he embraced an intellectual contradiction: a love of the wilderness and a faith in economic development and material progress.

Wisconsin, with fewer than five hundred students, was hardly a major university when Turner arrived in Madison. It was, however, an ideal place for an unusually bright, well-bred, highly motivated young man, even if he had to do some remedial work. Turner was prepared to make the most of the educational opportunities, but during the summer of 1879, he contracted spinal meningitis. Barely escaping death and physical impairment, he recovered his health at home and passed the hours by reading significant works of English and American literature. Returning to Madison, he enjoyed life in a social fraternity, edited the student newspaper, participated in college literary life, and won the coveted Burrows Prize for oratory—the highest honor the university could bestow on a student. Before big-time sports invaded campus life, the college orator, not the athlete, was the local hero. Robert La Follette, who had also won the Burrows Prize, used it as a springboard for his highly successful political career as leader of Wisconsin's Progressive Movement.

Far more important to Turner's future was his encounter with William Francis Allen, a remarkable professor of history. During his junior year at Wisconsin, Turner fell under Allen's spell. A New Englander educated in the classics at Harvard and broadly humanistic in outlook, Allen had studied in Berlin and Göttingen, where he had been thoroughly imbued with the new historical theories of Leopold von Ranke. No textbook teacher, Allen insisted that his students prepare original papers based on primary sources and utilize the scientific methods of the German school. Allen set Turner to work examining a French land grant. The result was not an earth-shattering study, but it demonstrated

solid training and sound scholarship based on original documents.[11] As important as initiating Turner in the methods of scientific historical scholarship was Allen's instilling in his student a
Darwinian view of material and cultural evolution. Turner embraced Allen's dynamic concept of institutional progress. He was
so deeply influenced by Allen that almost forty years later he
wrote, "Allen has always looked over my shoulder and stirred my
historical conscience."[12]

Graduated from the University of Wisconsin in 1884, Turner
flirted briefly with a career in journalism, but his whole life
changed when he accepted a job substituting for Allen, who took
a leave of absence. While he taught rhetoric and history in 1886,
Turner determined to make teaching his career and began work
on a Master of Arts degree. His thesis, "The Influence of the Fur
Trade in the Development of Wisconsin," was based on original
documents—many in French—in the State Historical Society of
Wisconsin. The society had already acquired a valuable collection
of frontier Americana. Overly optimistic, both his strength and
weakness, Turner thought he could complete the work quickly;
he did not finish the thesis until 1888. He also began a career as a
book reviewer for the popular press, a convenient way to earn
money, gain recognition, and express his enthusiasm for his
newfound scientific profession.[13]

President Thomas C. Chamberlain of the University of Wisconsin insisted that Turner further his education by working toward a doctorate at The Johns Hopkins University before he
could be considered for a permanent post in history. Turner en-
rolled in 1888 and entered one of the most demanding and rewarding periods of his life. Johns Hopkins was the premier
graduate institution in the nation, both in terms of the quality of
its faculty and of its graduate students. At Hopkins, Turner met
many of the historians and social scientists who would become the
lions of the profession of his generation: Woodrow Wilson, Richard T. Ely, Albion Small, Charles Homer Haskins, Charles

McLean Andrews, J. Franklin Jameson, and Herbert Baxter
Adams. They were heady company for a young man from Portage, but Turner earned the lasting respect and friendship of these
unusually gifted men.

At Hopkins the students and faculty worked with the fervor of
religious zealots. They were among the first generation of scien-
tifically trained professionals who wanted to create a new discipline based on research methods more rigorous than those of previous generations of American historians. They were well aware
of the writings of the best European scholars and understood
their influence on the Americans who were working with critical
skills in all fields of learning. Turner was virtually overwhelmed
by the smorgasbord of learning that was placed before him. The
Hopkins seminars brought together potential scholars from diverse disciplines.[14] The faculty sought to be appropriate professional role models, and the students tried to emulate them. In this
atmosphere, where no assumption was sacred and ideas were
commonly shared, freely discussed, and openly criticized, Turner
and his cohort thrived. His only suffering at Hopkins—slight at
that—was that he found little enthusiasm for his interest in the
early history of the West among the faculty and students, except
for Woodrow Wilson, himself the product of a small town.

Even the Johns Hopkins historians, however, were not free of
doctrine. Heidelberg-trained Herbert Baxter Adams, the leading
historian on the faculty, propounded the "germ theory," which
explained historical development in terms of "germs" or anteced-
ents. Adams saw little utility in studying early American institutions *per se;* in fact, he believed most of that work was already
done. He was more interested in seeking the origin of American
institutions in medieval Teutonic tribal structures. His approach
appealed to students of literature and law, in which Anglo-Saxon
linkages were critical. Turner believed that Adams actually
turned Americans away from looking at their recent past. At its
heart, the germ theory denied that anything meaningful or

unique could stem from the American experience of transplanted Europeans. Adams argued not so much for the continuity of history—something all historians accept—as against the idea that changed environments and circumstances could substantially alter institutions.[15] Turner's doctoral dissertation, an elaboration of his master's thesis, incorporated some of Adams's perspective by including a discussion of the fur trade in the ancient world, but Turner demonstrated that the Wisconsin experience was essentially different.

The young historian returned to Wisconsin in 1889 with a still uncertain future, but the premature death of his mentor, William Francis Allen, opened the way for a permanent appointment at the university in 1891. Wisconsin offered Turner an opportunity to demonstrate his skills and enthusiasm not only by contributing to the building of a great university but also by advancing the cause of the Hopkins method of historical studies. He shared President Chamberlain's desire to make the university the state's palladium. He advocated, also, Herbert Baxter Adams's belief that the university should reach out to the public through extension work, and he was among the first Wisconsin professors to give off-campus courses in history. Turner brought to the university both a sense of vision and a breadth of knowledge that made him a leader in the academic community. Despite the burdens of university service, Turner steadfastly built on the remarkable knowledge of politics, geography, economics, and sociology that he had acquired at Hopkins. He introduced his students to the materials in the State Historical Society of Wisconsin, worked alongside them, and continued to read widely.

In the 1891 *Wisconsin Journal of Education,* Turner published an essay, "The Significance of History" (the first essay in this volume), that he had presented as a talk to the Southwestern Wisconsin Teachers' Association. Although the circumstances of his writing the address and its subsequent reception are unclear, the invitation gave Turner a chance to spell out how history should be studied, how history should be written, and why history was important in a free society. Although the "Significance of History" may have been temporarily "buried" in an obscure magazine, it was an eloquent and pathbreaking piece that marked the direction of historical training, teaching, research, and writing for generations to come. Had Turner been a more distinguished scholar at the time, a member of the faculty at Harvard or Hopkins, his essay would doubtless have caused a stir in the profession; but as a younger man, comparatively unknown, and a professor at a "fresh water" university, Turner had to wait years before his ideas filtered into the profession. Only then did people recognize his primacy.

The "Significance of History" is so graciously written and so devoid of jargon that it is deceptively simple. There is no doubt that the essay reflected Turner's exposure during graduate school to the work of some the greatest modern historians. Richly illustrated with insightful quotations and historical examples, the talk must have impressed Turner's audience with his erudition. The essay, however, did more. Although Turner touched on many subjects, his main point was that history was neither a mindless chronicle of the past nor a mere branch of literature intended to entertain rather than educate readers; history is "all the remains that have come down to us from the past, studied with all the critical and interpretive power that the present can bring to the task."

Turner had little patience with authors who sacrificed truth for drama, who believed that history was merely one branch of literature or focussed exclusively on past politics, or who devoted their attention only to the behavior of powerful elites. The activities of the common people were equally important, Turner argued, and any gifted historian would look carefully into the lives of the "degraded tillers of the soil" to tell the true story. Although candid in his advocacy of progress, Turner pointed out that thoughtful history recounted tragedy as well as triumph and that the events in one part of the world often had unanticipated, even dire, consequences in distant lands. This was especially true of economic matters, for the modern world was so closely integrated that almost any action at one point of the globe could have profound ramifications for all others. Turner told his audience that the only way to understand the past was to recognize that it existed in a variety of contexts, and truth could only be gained by looking to the work of geographers, political scientists, economists, and theologians, whose research illuminated the past in ways as equally valid as those of historians. There were other contexts—myths, artifacts, folklore, and traditions—that warranted serious attention; the search for truth demanded a complete examination of as many sources as possible.

Turner also warned his listeners that no historian could write a definitive or final history. The scientific method, even in the hands of the most conscientious scholar, could not overcome an individual's cultural values, experience, and context. The greatest historians—from Herodotus and Thucydides to Hume and Carlyle—when seen in retrospect, proved to be advocates and partisans of interest groups and research methods that showed them to be creatures of their times. Turner's recognition of relativism in historical writing was a warning against the acceptance of orthodoxies and an advocation of the continuity and the unity of the past with the present. Local, state, and national history could be understood only in a world context. National history, when examined outside a global context, could degenerate into tribal history and shared its dangerous implications for promoting international conflict rather than world understanding.[16]

Unlike European nations, which valued their historians and placed them in important positions of government, Americans did not, Turner pointed out, except for the occasional appointment of a literary figure to a diplomatic post. Therefore, America's statesmen were not distinguished scholars, and the result, Turner insisted, was their obvious failure to understand do-

mestic and international problems or to debate them knowledge-
ably. The American public and their representatives must escape
this parochialism if they hoped to act wisely in the future. The
study of history would help broaden the nation's narrow hori-
zons. Equally important to the United States was that the study of
history was vital to the creation of the sense of citizenship so im-
perative to national development.

There is no doubt that during his early years at Wisconsin,
Turner had embarked on a most energetic reading program. His
notes and files indicate that little of major significance in relation
to American history was ignored.[17] He could follow leads from
one important work to another, and he had little fear of strug-
gling with books in foreign languages if he thought that they held
promise for his own interests.[18] This was a fertile and creative
period in Turner's life. In fact, Turner's biographer believes that
he displayed at this time a marked originality of thought, rebel-
liousness against convention, and inventiveness in methodology.[19]

The clearest manifestation of those characteristics was an essay
that Turner wrote for *The Ægis,* the University of Wisconsin's
undergraduate newspaper, in 1892. Entitled "Problems in American History," the essay identified many potential fields of study
but emphasized the two major ideas that were to dominate the
remainder of his life: the history of westward expansion and of
the sectional identities, conflicts, and compromises that resulted
from that expansion. Turner circulated copies of *The Ægis* article
among friends and colleagues, who gave it a cool to modest reception. Herbert Baxter Adams was the exception. Turner's mentor
was completely taken by the suggestive power of the piece and
asked Turner whether he would be willing to present a similar
evocative paper at the forthcoming meeting of the American Historical Association at the Chicago World's Fair.[20]

Turner agreed to the challenge but later offered to yield his
place to one of his students, Orin G. Libby. His proposal was re-
jected, and Turner began writing "The Significance of the Fron-

tier in American History" (the second essay in this volume), an essay that was to change his life and eventually place him in the vanguard of the profession. For some peculiar and yet-to-be-explained reason, historians have devoted years to seeking the sources of Turner's thought. They somehow imply that he lacked originality or primacy because he utilized materials he had read over the past years and absorbed "ideas that were in the air" among American and European intellectuals. Turner's warmest admirer insists that the ambitious young scholar used the works of others essentially to validate and document his own ideas; Turner himself could never adequately explain how the essay coalesced.[21] All of this scrutiny may be rewarding for scholarly purposes, but it misses the significance of Turner's essay. Turner both refocussed the way historians and, in fact, the general public were to look at the American past and evoked a century-long argument about the validity of his suggested interpretation of United States history.

There is irony in the fact that Herbert Baxter Adams, whose germ theory of history Turner displaced, was the individual who suggested his participation in the meeting. Little did Adams, or for that matter anyone else, anticipate the content of Turner's paper. Neither the audience that listened to Turner nor the scholars to whom he mailed published copies of the essay responded with noteworthy enthusiasm. Yet, before one decade passed, interest in the germ theory was superseded by frontier studies. Turner transformed the study of American institutions from the quest for their Teutonic origins, a subset of the expansion of Europe, into an independent field of study that spoke to scholars in other fields of history and researchers in other disciplines. It is unfair to Turner to argue that someone would have soon enough challenged the existing scheme for studying American history because the time had come for a major paradigmatic shift in emphasis. Turner did more than merely package current intellectual thought: "The Significance of the Frontier in American History" called for a dramatic break with the past. Despite Turner's earlier criticisms of writers who relied on literary and rhetorical techniques to bolster their arguments, the essay by its stylistic devices not only sustained its thesis but also gave it qualities that for a century made it a pleasure and joy to read.[22]

Turner began his essay by calling attention to a Bureau of the Census pamphlet pointing out that until 1890 the country had had a continuous frontier of settlement. However, the previously unsettled area, now widely broken into isolated bodies of settlement, no longer yielded a frontier line. The census report, combined with his past teaching and research, led Turner to ask the big question: What did the passing of the frontier mean to the United States? He then set out his own explanation: the "Turner thesis." The frontier experience of the American people had been a determining force in the creation of the nation's institutions and in the forging of its national character. The statement in the Bureau of the Census report marked the "closing of a great historic movement," Turner asserted; "Up to our own day American history has been in large degree the history of the colonization of the Great West."[23] He then went on to observe: "The existence of an area of free land . . . and the advance of American settlement westward explain American development." America's character resulted from the experience of a people who confronted "the changes involved in crossing a continent, in winning a wilderness, and in developing at each area of this progress, out of the primitive economic and political conditions of the frontier into the complexity of city life."

Turner's definition of the frontier was purposely vague. "The term is an elastic one," but the most significant thing about the frontier was that it was at the "hither edge of free land." It was also the "meeting point between savagery and civilization," and the site of the rapid Americanization of the population. He argued, too, that the critical function of the frontier was that it served as the site for the repeated rebirth of democratic institutions. American frontier democracy was unique because it was based on an egalitarian community, in which opportunity to begin again, to have another chance, existed for people from the East who were willing to confront the forces of nature.

Turner believed that the westering experience of the American people was at the heart of American exceptionalism. The westward movement was what made America and Americans different from Europe and Europeans. American characteristics—not all of them virtuous—resulted from the needs of a highly mobile population and the establishment of new communities. Cultural as well as physical baggage sometimes had to be shed by people when they faced a new environment. An American people that had been on the move for almost three hundred years, reacting repeatedly to the impact of the frontier, Turner remarked, were "strong in selfishness and individualism, intolerant of administrative experience and education," and eager to push individual liberty to its limits. Guilty of antisocial behavior and dubious ethics, frontier democracy provided examples of questionable economic and policy theories. Moreover, Turner traced American coarseness, strength, inquisitiveness, acquisitiveness, pragmatism, optimism, and lack of interest in aesthetics to a frontier past.

In associating political democracy with widespread landholding, Turner asserted that frontier democracy resulted from a more equitable distribution of economic opportunity than had been possible in any nation in the western world. The transformation of the American polity from Jeffersonian republicanism into the national republicanism of James Monroe and the popular democracy of Andrew Jackson was a process directly related to land distribution. Representing its landed origins, frontier political democracy demonstrated the venturesome spirit of the transient landed class of small proprietors rather than the subservience of a landless, immobile peasant class. Turner believed that the struggle between eastern economic interests and frontier settlers for the control and distribution of the economic resources on the frontier was a major issue in the nineteenth century. Turner's underscoring the intersectional character of economic questions was an implicit rejection of a class conflict interpretation of American history.[24]

Turner's seminal essay touched deep roots among American scholars. He provided a secular basis for American exceptionalism to replace the theological assertions of mid-nineteenth-century chauvinists. He argued that the Americans were a unique nationality, race, or people, as the term was used at the turn of the century. His arguments in favor of exceptionalism created an implicit leitmotif of both genuine pride and chauvinism. He asserted that the American identity originated neither in Puritan New England nor in the slave-holding South but on the moving frontier. He called attention also to the end of the pioneer epoch in American history. For Turner, by 1890, America had repeatedly replicated in a Darwinian sense the evolutionary process of change from a simple pastoral and extractive society into a complex urban and industrial organism. Muted in Turner's analysis were the voices of women, Indians, Mexican-Americans, and African-Americans, as well as other nonwhite people, but had Turner recognized or emphasized such factors as race and gender, he would have been an even more prescient historian.

Turner's essay, which admittedly reflected his own experience in part as someone who had grown to manhood in the shadow of the frontier, struck a sympathetic chord among state and local historians who were born, reared, or worked west of the Appalachians. For the first time, their research and writing could escape parochialism and find a place in the national narrative. It is little wonder that Turner made converts in the middle western and far western states. In 1895 he offered a course in the History of the West. Soon similar course offerings appeared in other school catalogues. Political scientists, economists, and geographers were quick to utilize the frontier thesis in their own studies.

A filtered version of the "Significance of the Frontier in

American History" gradually escaped from the academy and made its way into the marketplace of ideas, where it won increasing approval. In fact, the Frontier Thesis has achieved almost mythic dimensions. Novelists, playwrights, screenwriters, journalists, and politicians have expressed in various ways over the years Turner's ideas about the frontier narrative and, more especially, western—and by implication national—characteristics and traits. Even more interesting is that from the time James Bryce, the British ambassador to the United States, characterized the "West as the most American part of America,"[25] Europeans have held a bifurcated image of the United States as a land of great polyglot cities but also of a Turnerian West of individualism, free land, and opportunity.[26]

In the years following the publication of his essay, Turner emerged as a leader in the historical profession. He was a confidant of J. Franklin Jameson, editor of the *American Historical Review,* and an advisor to the Historical Division of the Carnegie Institution, which was managed by Jameson. Turner continued to write and publish. His syllabi, scholarly essays, and popular articles appeared regularly. He published a stimulating analytical history, *The Rise of the New West, 1819–1829,* that further enhanced his reputation. By 1910 Turner had a distinguished vita. He had not only edited the correspondence of the French ministers to the United States during the 1790s and written encyclopedia articles, innovative scholarly essays, critical book reviews, and a monograph, but he had also produced what was recognized even then as the most famous essay ever written by an American historian. In 1910 he was president of the American Historical Association.

As Turner's influence grew within the profession, his status in the University of Wisconsin increased. He played a key role in the development of the university's Department of History, which became one of the nation's premier graduate training centers in the field. He was a faculty spokesman on issues of academic free-

dom. Although he was certainly the best-known Wisconsin historian outside the university, the other members of the faculty
helped to raise the department to an enviable level of excellence
that continued long after Turner left.

Turner's failure to produce his major work, his repeated re-
quests for increased release time from teaching, and his role in the
faculty brought him into conflict with the University of Wisconsin Board of Regents. He waged an unsuccessful campaign
against the abuses of intercollegiate football. He objected to the
intrusive role that the university regents played in departmental
affairs. He fought an unending struggle against regents who
wanted to de-emphasize research in the humanities in favor of
agriculture and science. Turner, blessed many times over with
invitations from Berkeley, Stanford, and Harvard, decided that
only his departure might shock the regents into recognizing that
they were out of step with the march of higher education in the
United States. After Turner left Wisconsin for Harvard, the regents did yield. They granted the university faculty a level of academic freedom and self-governance that was to make Wisconsin
a model institution of higher learning.

Turner moved to Harvard in 1910 partly because the school
made the best offer and partly because he was tired of "pioneer-
ing" for western history.[27] He found the Harvard Department of
History congenial if not entirely friendly, his students able, but
much work to be done on behalf of western history.[28] Turner's
position as a senior member of the profession was assured, and he
was much sought after to lecture and to advise. In fact his role as
part of the establishment of the American Historical Association
drew fire from a rebellious group of historians who wanted the
organization democratized.[29] Between the affairs of the association and the coming of the First World War, Turner's research
suffered. Although an anti-interventionist during the early days
of the war, patriotism and intense hostility to the divisive spirit
among hyphenated Americans led Turner to join the National

Board of Historical Services, but his role was minimal. Turner was not a great propagandist; he believed serious historians setting forth the facts could counteract the misunderstandings that might harm the people's morale by clouding the nation's war aims in the conflict.

When Turner published his essay, "Problems in American History" in *The Ægis,* he marked out two areas for study: westward expansion and sectionalism. The first he dealt with one year later in "The Significance of the Frontier in American History." This intuitive construction of national development was not based on extensive research; in fact, it was a call for others to examine the past in a new light. Turner himself, although justly proud of the Frontier Thesis, never undertook a grand synthesis of American history within that paradigm.

The presentation of his ideas about sectionalism evolved quite differently.[30] Turner's interest in sectionalism dated from his student days. Very early on, Turner began to gather data and read extensively the works of scholars in other disciplines, especially geography. The late nineteenth and early twentieth centuries witnessed a flowering of physical geography and cartography, and Turner had access to the work of some the field's most creative thinkers. Geographers throughout the western world were already trying to correlate economic, social, and political structures to regional environments. There is no doubt that Turner was familiar with the works of men like Friedrich Ratzel, John Wesley Powell, and Charles Van Hise. But Turner never became a geographic determinist. He made extensive use of census reports, voting statistics, literary works, agricultural reports, demographic data, and historical studies.[31] For example, Turner's definition of a section leaned very heavily on philosopher Josiah Royce's Phi Beta Kappa talk on "Provincialism," which stressed the primacy of culture in the defining of sections, or regions. Turner repeatedly told his students that the United States consisted of congeries of sections and that its history is the

outcome of the interaction of these various regions.[32]   Since
Turner organized his research materials with extreme care and
wrote extensively on the subject both in theoretical articles and in
scholarly monographs—modifying, and expanding his perspective—historians have had little difficulty in tracing the evolution
of his thought.

In 1906 Turner published *The Rise of the New West, 1819–1829*,
the first treatment of American history that recognized both the
frontier and sectionalism. His study examined the creation of several regional identities within the nation. Focussing on the leading political and economic issues of the decade, he demonstrated
that responses to them were not merely conflicts between the
North and the South but that sections were dynamic social, cultural, political, and economic entities. While some areas of the
West gradually changed over time, from West to North or South,
others did not. The so-called Era of Good Feeling merely masked
a major restructuring of political life based more closely on sectional economic and social realities. Turner's highly analytical sectional approach won uniform approval from reviewers, but historians remained skeptical of the feasibility of an overall regional
history.

Following the publication of *The Rise of the New West,* Turner
decided to launch a follow-up volume covering the years 1830 to
1850—what he called "THE BOOK"—and to promote his sectional
thesis before scholarly audiences. In 1907 he presented a paper
before the American Sociological Association in Madison with
the challenging title, "Is Sectionalism Dying Away?" Turner argued that in the postfrontier era, the interests of the settled sections of the nation would eclipse the more local concerns of the
states and would form the basis on which conflicting economic
and political interests would be resolved. Sociologists proved as
reluctant as historians to accept Turner's paradigm. Turner made
a much more plausible case for sectionalism in a shrewdly constructed essay entitled "The Old West," which pointed to the re-

gionally based difference between the coastal lowlands and the upcountry. "The Old West" won almost instant approval and remains an interesting piece of work despite subsequent historical revisionism.[33] Turner was on firmer ground when he wrote monographic historical pieces; his theoretical essays usually sparked controversy, except when he spoke to geographers, who greeted them enthusiastically.[34]

Over the years Turner was disappointed that his pleas for a greater appreciation of the geographical influences on American history were generally unheeded, but he continued to write papers with sectional themes. He plugged away at gathering data for THE BOOK, which would be, he hoped, a major contribution to the field of American history. In 1918 he was invited to give a series of lectures at Boston's Lowell Institute. Still deeply attached to the idea that geographic regions influenced people's lives, he argued that the section was like a nation in the European community. In the United States sections were held together by the cohesive force of political parties whose shared interests crossed regional lines. When political parties failed to exert common interests across regions, when sectional and party interests coincided and links with other sections could not be forged, as occurred during the 1850s, civil war rather than peaceful compromise resulted. Turner had hoped that drafting the lectures would aid his writing THE BOOK, but they only proved the need for deeper research and clearer conceptualization than what he had achieved to that time.

Poor health forced Turner into an early retirement from Harvard. He left Cambridge for Madison, where he planned to live near his family. He felt like "a pioneer in a new clearing."[35] His goal was to finish the sectional book, but Turner had never been an effective manager of money, and financial considerations forced him into accepting speaking engagements and even teaching a short course at Wisconsin, all of which delayed his work. When invited to be the featured speaker at the January 1925 meeting of the State Historical Society of Wisconsin, Turner believed he could not refuse. Moreover, the engagement would offer another opportunity to make his case for the sectional thesis in a revised form.

Turner's new version, "The Significance of the Section in American History" (the third essay in this volume), was based on his original idea: The expanding frontier led to intersectional conflicts that continued into the postfrontier era; and the nature of the space in which a people lived influenced their institutions. But the revised essay was a mature one that reflected the many changes in the world since the publication of his "Problems" essay in 1892. To illustrate his arguments, Turner produced a host of examples from a quotation by Cotton Mather about people who had "got unto the *Wrong side of the Hedge*" to one by Boston mayor James Curley who opposed the Great Lakes-St. Lawrence Seaway project because it "would obliterate New England absolutely." The First World War and the quest for a League of Nations also affected him. He continued his previously stated argument that American sectional rivalries were like those of European nations but that, within each section, dissenting minorities found allies in other sections. Intersectional agreements nurtured a sustained national consensus.

Some ideas in the Sectional Thesis were new or received greater stress. Turner defended the value of the section or province—he quoted from Josiah Royce—as a bulwark against nationalizing trends that would threaten the local sense of community. But Turner also warned that no section should believe its culture is superior to another section's culture and that no section should try to impose its culture on another section. The elasticity of political parties, he hoped, would defend against such dangers. In addition he stressed the role of urbanization in American life. Cities, by their nature, could upset normal sectional interests.

Even more important was that Turner expressed the concern of the neo-Malthusians about the rapidly diminishing resources and the rising population of the nation. The forest, food, and mineral resource base of the nation was shrinking, and conflict over how best to use it was also divisive. What would happen if the nation could no longer grow enough food to feed itself? The agricultural base must be preserved, even at the expense of urban growth.

The American party system and the spirit of the common good that existed among the nation's great statesmen, Turner believed, had served the nation well. He backed away from geographic determinism by admitting that a section resulted from the joint influence of its geology and its colonizing stock. Sections, Turner argued, would not fade away because they had particular ideals and interests. They should be studied because they have shaped and will continue to shape the lives of Americans.

If Turner had hoped that his essay would evoke the kind of dialogue and have the influence that his frontier piece did years earlier, he was disappointed. Even friends who praised his Sectional Thesis found little that was new. He had more luck with a talk to geographers given later in the year.[36] Shortly thereafter Merle Curti and Arthur M. Schlesinger, historians whose opinions he valued, also wrote approvingly of his sectional ideas. Turner probably could not have anticipated that what was most obvious in his Sectional Thesis would be the most lasting and what he thought to be most subtle would be slighted. His belief that intersectional rivalry would increase but be modified by political parties may be true in a general way, but sectional rivalry is certainly not a significant force in history. Yet, Turner's idea of regional identities, however blurred, has grown stronger, if not in a political way, then certainly in a cultural sense.[37] He was correct when he asserted that the West is as much a region as the North or the South. Moreover, modern demographers, ethnographers, sociologists, and folklorists have taken regionalism quite seriously. Turner recognized and pioneered the need to study regional distinctions. Unfortunately, because of his methodologies and his biases, his work is today little acknowledged as the proper cornerstone of the field.

Retirement did not seem to hold a promising future for Turner. He knew that his Sectional Thesis would not gain acceptance until he finished THE BOOK. Turner returned to his research, lectures, and essays. The severity of the Wisconsin winters and straitened financial circumstances took a toll on him and limited his productivity.

In 1927 salvation came in the form of an invitation from his old friend Max Farrand to move to southern California and join the staff of the Huntington Library. Farrand, the library's director of research, and George Ellery Hale, of the California Institute of Technology, convinced the Huntington trustees that Turner would bring prestige to the fledgling research center. A generous salary removed all of his financial problems, and Turner was given freedom to consult with the library's staff, to complete his research, and to write THE BOOK.

Turner began to write and rewrite, although plagued by failing health. Aided by a secretary, he worked steadily on the sectional book, which at one time seemed like the beginning of a two-volume opus. He also selected a dozen of his essays for republication, but he did not live long enough to see the collection in print. He died March 24, 1932. The book of essays, entitled *The Significance of Sections in American History,* was a companion volume to a collection of essays Turner had published in 1920, *The Frontier in American History.* The former's key essay was his talk at the Wisconsin State Historical Society. Allan Nevins, who was to emerge as one of the leading American historians of his generation, called the book to the attention of Mark DeWolfe Howe. As a member of the Pulitzer Prize committee, Howe read the book, and it received the Pulitzer Prize in 1933.[38]

THE BOOK, which Turner left unfinished, was completed through the dedicated effort of Turner's student, Avery Craven, and his secretary, Merrill Crissey. Their task was almost impossible, but after several years they had a volume that represented not only the state of learning at the time of Turner's death but also filled in his basic outlines. Published in 1935 under the title, *The United States, 1830–1850: The Nation and Its Sections,* their book probably came close to what Turner had in mind. Had the book been published a quarter of a century earlier, had it enjoyed Turner's final factual and stylistic revisions, and had it encountered a readership not in the grip of a worldwide economic depression, Turner's work may have been challenged but would have been more appreciated. In the 1930s the book seemed dated, addressing forgotten issues. Even the hard work of Craven and Crissey could not overcome its inherent structural and conceptual flaws. Nevertheless, it remains an evocative book filled with interesting insights and subjects warranting additional research.

As a young man, and even in his mature years, Turner was a historian known for "bright ideas" rather than one who simply reworked a particular era, wrote textbooks, turned out monographs, or edited documents. He had the skills to perform these tasks, and on occasion used them, except that the textbook always eluded him. Turner was a gifted researcher and an inspirational teacher, especially for graduate students because he sparkled with topics for study. Generations of scholars have found his paradigm for understanding the nineteenth century useful. The essay was his best literary vehicle. The three that follow, each reprinted verbatim from its original source, may yet elicit surprise and pleasure, for Turner tried to see American history as something more than mere dead words on the page. He knew that each generation wrote its own history, and he would have been pleased to know that his essays still play a role in ours.

Notes

1. For an introduction to the literature dealing with Frederick Jackson Turner, see Vernon E. Mattson and William E. Marion, *Frederick Jackson Turner: A Reference Guide* (Boston: G. K. Hall & Co., 1985); and Gerald D. Nash, *Creating the West: Historical Interpretations, 1890–1990* (Albuquerque: University of New Mexico Press, 1991).

2. For a perceptive analysis of Turner's views on sectionalism, see Michael D. Steiner, "The Significance of Turner's Sectional Thesis," *Western Historical Quarterly* 10 (October 1979), 437–66.

3. For a discussion of why Turner, but no other American historian, has earned such distinction, see Martin Ridge, "The Life of an Idea: The Significance of Frederick Jackson Turner's Frontier Thesis," *Montana: The Magazine of Western History* 40 (Winter 1991), 3–13.

4. For the most careful analysis of Turner's critics and the context in which they wrote, see Nash, *Creating the West.*

5. For implicit criticism of this kind, see Richard White, "Frederick Jackson Turner," in John R. Wunder, ed., *Historians of the American Frontier* (New York: Greenwood Press, 1988), 660–81.

6. See Martin Ridge, "Frederick Jackson Turner and His Ghost: The Writing of Western History," *Proceedings* of the American Antiquarian Society 101 (April 1991), 65–76; and Glenda Riley's review of Richard White's *"It's Your Misfortune and None of My Own": A New History of the American West,* in the *Western Historical Quarterly* 13 (May 1992), 223–25. Riley observes, "The 'new' western historians are as tied to Frederick Jackson Turner as the 'old'; they dispute him, rewrite him, and disprove." Ibid., p. 225.

7. Michael C. Steiner, "Frederick Jackson Turner and Western Regionalism," in Richard Etulain, ed., *Writing Western History* (Albuquerque: University of New Mexico Press, 1991), 103–35. See also Merrill Jensen, ed., *Regionalism in America* (Madison: University of Wisconsin Press, 1951).

8. The best source for Turner's life is Ray Allen Billington, *Frederick Jackson Turner: Historian, Scholar, Teacher* (New York: Oxford University Press, 1973), but one should not overlook the interpretive biographical sketch in Wilbur R. Jacobs, *Frederick Jackson Turner's Legacy: Unpublished Writings in American History* (San Marino: Huntington Library, 1965).

9. Frederick Jackson Turner to Joseph Schafer, October 14, 1931, Turner Papers, Henry E. Huntington Library, San Marino, California.

10. It is worth remembering that Turner's experiences were scarcely unique among intellectuals. He was the contemporary of John Muir, Thorstein Veblen, and Hamlin Garland, all of whom were reared in rural Wisconsin.

11. It was later published as "History of the 'Grignon Tract' on the Portage of the Fox and the Wisconsin Rivers," Portage *State Register,* June 23, 1883.

12. Turner to Carl Becker, October 26, 1920, Turner Papers.

13. For a study of Turner as a reviewer, see Martin Ridge, "A More Jealous Mistress: Frederick Jackson Turner as a Book Reviewer," *Pacific Historical Review* 55 (February 1986), 49–63.

14. Shortly before Turner's arrival at Hopkins, the California-born philosopher,

Josiah Royce, later a leading figure in American thought, came to Hopkins after studying in Germany. Royce participated in Herbert Baxter Adams's "seminary" on history and politics, where he read a paper on Spinoza, so wide ranging were the topics of discussion. Robert V. Hine, *Josiah Royce: From Grass Valley to Harvard* (Norman: University of Oklahoma Press, 1992), 94.

15. Herbert Baxter Adams was far more open than is often suggested. He not only allowed but encouraged his students to look at all dimensions of American history, including contemporary subjects. See Billington, *Frederick Jackson Turner,* 74.

16. There is no little irony in the fact that Turner, often denounced for advocating a chauvinistic and apologetic history for the United States, argued most persuasively against tribalism.

17. Turner's reading during this period has been of immense interest to scholars dealing with his intellectual development. They have sought out every possible source for his ideas. There are convenient summaries of this literature in Billington, *Genesis of the Frontier Thesis: A Study in Historical Creativity* (San Marino: Huntington Library, 1971), and especially Jacobs, *Frederick Jackson Turner's Legacy.*

18. See for example, Lee Benson's essay, "Achille Loria's Influence on American Economic Thought, Including his Contributions to the Frontier Hypothesis," *Agricultural History* 24 (October 1949), 182–99.

19. Billington, *Frederick Jackson Turner,* 106.

20. Herbert Baxter Adams to Turner, November 28, 1892, Turner Papers.

21. Billington, *Frederick Jackson Turner,* 124.

22. For an insightful analysis of Turner's rhetoric and the role it played in the development of his famous essay, see Ronald H. Carpenter, *The Eloquence of Frederick Jackson Turner* (San Marino: Huntington Library, 1983). Both Turner's critics and defenders have described Turner's early essays as poetic.

23. Years later Turner observed: "Occasionally, I think I have been careless in using the phrase 'frontier ending' for 'line of frontier ending'; but I have always realized that there was a difference and that the frontier did not come to an end 'with a bang' in 1890." Turner to Frederick Merk, January 9, 1931, Turner Papers.

24. Charles A. Beard, who provided the first economic interpretation of American history, was initially a harsh critic of Turner's adoption of sectional rather than class analysis but later praised him as giving stature to economic history. Beard wrote, "Mr. Turner deserves everlasting credit for his services as the leader in restoring the consideration of economic facts to historical writing in America." Charles A. Beard to Merle Curti, August 9, 1928, Turner Papers.

25. James Bryce, *The American Commonwealth* (Chicago: Charles H. Sergel & Co., 1891), II, 697.

26. Ridge, "The Life of an Idea," 12–13; Nash, *Creating the West,* 197–257.

27. Turner to Max Farrand, October 28, 1909, Turner Papers.

28. For Turner's role in raising money for his western history program and his unique relationship with a patron, see Ray Allen Billington, ed., *"Dear Lady": The Letters of Frederick Jackson Turner and Alice Forbes Perkins Hooper, 1910–1932* (San Marino: Huntington Library, 1970).

29. Ray Allen Billington, "Tempest in Clio's Teapot: The American Historical

Association's Rebellion of 1915," *American Historical Review* 78 (April 1973), 348–69.

30. For a succinct discussion of the origin and development of Turner's thought, see Steiner, "Frederick Jackson Turner and Western Regionalism," 103–35.

31. For an analysis of the sources available to Turner before 1900, see Billington, *Frederick Jackson Turner,* 210–16.

32. Ibid., 216.

33. Frederick Jackson Turner, "The Old West," *Proceedings* of the Wisconsin State Historical Society 26 (1908), 184–233.

34. For example, Turner's 1914 essay, "Geographic Influences in American History" received a warm reception at the joint meeting of the Association of American Geographers and the American Geographical Society; but his "Significance of Sections in American History," presented to the American Historical Association the same year, was so poorly received that Turner refused to publish it.

35. Turner to Dorothy Turner Main, May 28, 1924, Turner Papers.

36. Frederick Jackson Turner, "Geographical Sectionalism in American History," *Annals* of the Association of American Geographers 16 (June 1926), 85–93.

37. Steiner, "The Significance of Turner's Sectional Thesis," 437–66.

38. Turner's biographer states that the Pulitzer Prize honored Turner for his previous work. Billington, *Frederick Jackson Turner,* 417.

Portage, Wisconsin, 1856.
(Courtesy, State Historical Society of Wisconsin, WHi(X3)38826.)

Portage, Wisconsin, ca. 1870.
(Courtesy, State Historical Society of Wisconsin, WHi(X3)34870.)

Frederick Jackson Turner was a freshman at the University of
Wisconsin when this photograph was taken in 1881.
(Courtesy, State Historical Society of Wisconsin, WHi(X3)883.)

Professor William F. Allen of the University of Wisconsin and
his son Will in the study of their home at 228 Langdon Street,
Madison, Wisconsin.

(Courtesy, State Historical Society of Wisconsin, WHi(X3)18013.)

Professor Frederick Jackson Turner conducting an
American history seminar in an alcove of the Wisconsin
Historical Society's library in the State Capitol
during the 1893–1894 academic year.
(Courtesy, State Historical Society of Wisconsin, WHi(X3)46720.)

Frederick Jackson Turner, ca. 1900–1905.
(Courtesy, State Historical Society of Wisconsin, WHi(X3)22894.)

Frederick Jackson Turner, the avid outdoorsman.
(Courtesy, State Historical Society of Wisconsin, WHi(X3)3211.)

Frederick Jackson Turner at Hancock Point, Maine, ca. 1927.
(Courtesy, State Historical Society of Wisconsin, WHi(X3)1185.)

Frederick Jackson Turner, December 1917.
(Courtesy, State Historical Society of Wisconsin, WHi(X3)1354.)

Each age writes the history of the past with reference to the conditions uppermost in its own time.

But the most important effect of the frontier has been in the promotion of democracy here and in Europe.

There is a geography of political habit——a geography of opinion, of material interest, of racial stock, of physical fitness, of social traits, of literature, of the distribution of men of ability, even of religious denomination.

History,
Frontier,
and Section

FREDERICK JACKSON TURNER

The Significance
of History

THE CONCEPTIONS OF HISTORY have been almost as numerous as the men who have written history. To Augustine Birrell history is a pageant; it is for the purpose of satisfying our curiosity. Under the touch of a literary artist the past is to become living again. Like another Prospero the historian waves his wand, and the deserted streets of Palmyra sound to the tread of artisan and officer, warrior gives battle to warrior, ruined towers rise by magic, and the whole busy life of generations that have long ago gone down to dust comes to life again in the pages of a book. The artistic prose narration of past events—this is the ideal of those who view history as literature. To this class belong romantic literary artists who strive to give to history the coloring and dramatic action of fiction, who do not hesitate to paint a character blacker or whiter than he really was, in order that the interest of the page may be increased, who force dull facts into vivacity, who create impressive situations, who, in short, strive to realize as an ideal the success of Walter Scott. It is of the historic Froude that Freeman says: "The most winning style, the choicest metaphors, the neatest phrases from foreign tongues would all be thrown away if they were devoted to proving that any two sides of a triangle are not always greater than the third side. When they are devoted to proving that a man cut off his wife's head one day and married her maid the next morning out of sheer love for his country, they win believers for the paradox." It is of the reader of this kind of history that Seeley writes: "To him, by some magic, parliamentary debates shall be always lively, officials always men of strongly marked, interesting character. There shall be nothing to remind him of the blue-book or the law book, nothing common or prosaic; but he shall sit as in a theater and gaze at splendid scenery and costume. He shall never be called upon to study or to judge, but only to imagine and enjoy. His reflections, as he reads, shall be precisely those of the novel reader; he shall ask: Is this character well drawn? is it really amusing? is the interest of the story well sustained, and does it rise properly toward the close?"

But after all these criticisms we may gladly admit that in itself an interesting style, even a picturesque manner of presentation, is not to be condemned, provided that truthfulness of substance rather than vivacity of style be the end sought. But granting that a man may be the possessor of a good style which he does not allow to run away with him, either in the interest of the artistic impulse or in the cause of party, still there remain differences as to the aim and method of history. To a whole school of writers, among whom we find some of the great historians of our time, history is the study of politics, that is, in the high signification given the word of Aristotle, as meaning all that concerns the activity of the state itself. "History is past politics and politics present history," says the great author of the *Norman Conquest*. Maurenbrecher of Leipzig speaks in no less certain tones: "The bloom of historical studies is the history of politics;" and Lorenz of Jena asserts: "The proper field of historical investigation, in the closer sense of the word, is politics." Says Seeley: "The modern historian works at the same task as Aristotle in his Politics." "To study history is to study not merely a narrative but at the same time certain theoretical studies." "To study history is to study problems." And thus a great circle of profound investigators, with true scientific method, have expounded the evolution of political institutions, studying their growth as the biologist might study seed, bud, blossom, and fruit. The results of these labors may be seen in such monumental works as those of Waitz on German institutions, Stubbs on English constitutional history, and Maine on early institutions.

There is another and an increasing class of historians to whom history is the study of the economic growth of the people, who aim to show that property, the distribution of wealth, the social conditions of the people, are the underlying and determining factors to be studied. This school, whose advance guard was led by Roscher, having already transformed orthodox political economy by its historical method, is now going on to rewrite history from the economic point of view. Perhaps the best English expression of the ideas of the school is to be found in Thorold Rogers' *Economic Interpretation of History*. He asserts truly that "very often the cause of great political events and great social movements is economical and has hitherto been undetected." So important does the fundamental principle of this school appear to me that I desire to quote from Mr. Rogers a specific illustration of this new historical method.

"In the twelfth and thirteenth centuries [he writes] there were numerous and well frequented routes from the markets of Hindustan to the Western world, and for the conveyance of that Eastern produce which was so greatly desired as a seasoning to the coarse and often unwholesome diet of our forefathers. The principal ports to which this produce was conveyed were Seleucia (latterly called Licia) in the Levant, Trebizond, and the Black Sea, and Alexandria. From these ports this Eastern produce was collected mainly by the Venetian and Genoese traders and conveyed over the passes of the Alps to the upper Danube and the Rhine. Here it was a source of great wealth to the cities which we planted on these waterways, from Ratisbon and Nuremberg to Bruges and Antwerp. The stream of commerce was not deep nor broad, but it was singularly fertilizing, and everyone who has any knowledge of the only history worth knowing knows how important these cities were in the later Middle Ages.

"In the course of time, all but one of these routes had been blocked by the savages who desolated central Asia, and still desolate it. It was therefore the object of the most enterprising of the Western nations to get, if possible, in the rear of these destructive brigands, by discovering a long sea passage to Hindustan. All Eastern trade depended on the Egyptian road being kept open, and this remaining road was already threatened. The beginning of this discovery was the work of a Portuguese prince. The expedition of Columbus was an attempt to discover a passage to India over the Western sea. By a curious coincidence the Cape passage was doubled, and the new world discovered almost simultaneously.

"The discoveries were made none too soon. Selim I (1512–20), the sultan of Turkey, conquered Mesopotamia and the holy towns of Arabia, and annexed Egypt during his brief reign. This conquest blocked the only remaining road which the Old World knew. The thriving manufactures of Alexandria were at once destroyed. Egypt ceased to be the highway from Hindustan. I discovered that some cause must be at work which had hitherto been unsuspected in the sudden and enormous rise of prices in all Eastern products, at the close of the first quarter of the sixteenth century, and found that it must have come from the conquest of Egypt. The river of commerce was speedily dried up. The cities which had thriven on it were gradually ruined, at least so far as this source of their wealth was concerned, and the trade of the Danube and Rhine ceased. The Italian cities fell into rapid decay. The German nobles, who had got themselves incorporated among the burghers of the free cities, were impoverished, and betook themselves the obvious expedient of reimbursing their losses by the pillage of their tenants. Then came the Peasants' War, its ferocious incidents, its cruel suppression, and the development of those wild sects which disfigured and arrested the German Reformation. The battle of the Pyramids, in which Selim gained the sultanate of Egypt for the Osmanli Turks, brought loss and misery into thousands of homes where the event had never been heard of. It is such facts as these which the economic interpretation of history illustrates and expounds."

Viewed from this position, the past is filled with new meaning. The focal point of modern interest is the fourth estate, the great mass of the people. History has been a romance and a tragedy. In it we read the brilliant annals of the few. The intrigues of courts, knightly valor, palaces and pyramids, the loves of ladies, the songs of minstrels, and the chants from cathedrals pass like a pageant, or linger like a strain of music as we turn the pages. But history has its tragedy as well, which tells of the degraded tillers of the soil, toiling that others might dream, the slavery that rendered possible the "glory that was Greece," the serfdom into which decayed the "grandeur that was Rome"—these as well demand their annals. Far oftener than has yet been shown have these underlying economic facts affecting the breadwinners of the nation been the secret of the nation's rise or fall, by the side of which much that has passed as history is the merest frippery.

But I must not attempt to exhaust the list of the conceptions of history. To a large class of writers, represented by Hume, the field of historical writing is an arena, whereon are to be fought out present partisan debates. Whig is to struggle against Tory, and the party of the writer's choice is to be victorious at whatever cost to the truth. We do not lack these partisan historians in America. To Carlyle, the hero-worshipper, history is the stage on which a few great men play their parts. To Max Müller history is the exposition of the growth of religious ideas. To the moralist history is the text whereby to teach a lesson. To the metaphysician history is the fulfillment of a few primary laws.

Plainly we may make choice from among many ideals. If, now, we strive to reduce them to some kind of order, we find that in each age a different ideal of history has prevailed. To the savage history is the painted scalp, with its symbolic representations of the victims of his valor; or it is the legend of the gods and heroes of his race—attempts to explain the origin of things. Hence the vast body of mythologies, folklore, and legends, in which science, history, fiction, are all blended together, judgment and imagination inextricably confused. As time passes the artistic instinct comes in, and historical writing takes the form of the Iliad, or the Nibelungenlied. Still we have in these writings the reflection of the imaginative, credulous age that believed in the divinity of its heroes and wrote down what it believed. Artistic and critical faculty find expression in Herodotus, father of Greek history, and in Thucydides, the ideal Greek historian. Both write from the standpoint of an advanced civilization and strive to present a real picture of the events and an explanation of the causes of the events. But Thucydides is a Greek; literature is to him an art, and history a part of literature; and so it seems to him no violation of historical truth to make his generals pronounce long orations that were composed for them by the historian. Moreover, early men and Greeks alone believed their own tribe or state to be the favored of the gods: the rest of humanity was for the most part outside the range of history.

To the medieval historian history was the annals of the monastery, or the chronicle of court and camp.

In the nineteenth century a new ideal and method of history arose. Philosophy prepared the way for it. Schelling taught the doctrine "that the state is not in reality governed by laws of man's devising, but is a part of the moral order of the universe, ruled by cosmic forces from above." Herder proclaimed the doctrine of growth in human institutions. He saw in history the development of given germs; religions were to be studied by comparison and by tracing their origins from superstitions up toward rational conceptions of God. Language, too, was no sudden creation, but a growth, and was to be studied as such; and so with political institutions. Thus he paved the way for the study of comparative philology, of mythology, and of political evolution. Wolf, applying Herder's suggestions to the Iliad, found no single Homer as its author, but many. This led to the critical study of the texts. Niebuhr applied this mode of study to the Roman historians and proved their incorrectness. Livy's history of early Rome became legend. Then Niebuhr tried to find the real facts. He believed that, although the Romans had forgotten their own history, still it was possible by starting with institutions of known reality to construct their predecessors, as the botanist may infer bud from flower. He would trace causes from effects. In other words, so strongly did he believe in the growth of an institution according to fixed laws that he believed he could reconstruct the past, reaching the real facts even by means of the incorrect accounts of the Roman writers.

Although he carried his method too far, still it was the foundation of the modern historical school. He strove to reconstruct old Rome as it really was out of the original authorities that remained. By critical analysis and interpretation he attempted so to use these texts that the buried truth should come to light. To skill as an antiquary he added great political insight—for Neibuhr was a practical statesman. It was his aim to unite critical study of the materials with the interpretative skill of the political expert, and this has been the aim of the new school of historians. Leopold von Ranke applied this critical method to the study of modern history. To him a document surviving from the past itself was of far greater value than any amount of tradition regarding the past. To him the contemporary account, rightly used, was of far higher authority than the second-hand relation. And so he searched diligently in the musty archives of European courts, and the result of his labors and those of his scholars has been the rewriting of modern diplomatic and political history. Charters, correspondence, contemporary chronicles, inscriptions, these are the materials on which he and his disciples worked. To "tell things as they really were" was Ranke's ideal. But to him, also, history was primarily past politics.

Superficial and hasty as this review has been, I think you see that the historical study of the first half of the nineteenth century reflected the thought of that age. It was an age of political agitation and inquiry, as our own age still so largely is. It was an age of science. That inductive study of phenomena which has worked a revolution in our knowledge of the external world was applied to history. In a word, the study of history became scientific and political.

Today the questions that are uppermost and that will become

increasingly important, are not so much political as economic questions. The age of machinery, of the factory system, is also the age of socialistic inquiry.

It is not strange that the predominant historical study is coming to be the study of past social conditions, inquiry as to landholding, distribution of wealth, and the economic basis of society in general. Our conclusion, therefore, is that there is much truth in all these conceptions of history: history is past literature, it is past politics, it is past religion, it is past economics.

Each age tries to form its own conception of the past. *Each age writes the history of the past anew with reference to the conditions uppermost in its own time.* Historians have accepted the doctrine of Herder. Society grows. They have accepted the doctrine of Comte. Society is an organism. History is the biography of society in all its departments. There is objective history and subjective history. Objective history applies to the events themselves; subjective history is man's conception of these events. "The whole mode and manner of looking at things alters with every age," but this does not mean that the real events of a given age change; it means that our comprehension of these facts changes.

History, both objective and subjective, is ever *becoming,* never completed. The centuries unfold to us more and more the meaning of past times. Today we understand Roman history better than did Livy or Tacitus, not only because we know how to use the sources better but also because the significance of events develops with time, because today is so much a product of yesterday that yesterday can only be understood as it is explained by today. The aim of history, then, is to know the elements of the present by understanding what came into the present from the past. For the present is simply the developing past, the past the undeveloped present. As well try to understand the egg without a knowledge of its developed form, the chick, as to try to understand the past without bringing to it the explanation of the present; and equally well try to understand an animal without study of its embryology as to understand one's time without study of the events that went before. The antiquarian strives to bring back the past for the sake of the past; the historian strives to show the present to itself by revealing its origin from the past. The goal of the antiquarian is the dead past; the goal of the historian is the living present. Droysen has put this true conception into the statement, "History is the 'Know Thyself' of humanity—the self-consciousness of mankind."

If, now, you accept with me the statement of this great master of historical science, the rest of our way is clear. If history be, in truth, the self-consciousness of humanity, the "self-consciousness of the living age, acquired by understanding its development from the past," all the rest follows.

First we recognize why all the spheres of man's activity must be considered. Not only is this the only way in which we can get a complete view of the society, but not one department of social life can be understood in isolation from the others. The economic life and the political life touch, modify, and condition one another. Even the religious life needs to be studied in conjunction with the political and economic life, and vice versa. Therefore all kinds of history are essential—history as politics, history as art, history as economics, history as religion—all are truly parts of society's endeavor to understand itself by understanding its past.

Next we see that history is not shut up in a book—not in many books. The first lesson the student of history has to learn is to discard his conception that there are standard ultimate histories. In the nature of the case this is impossible. *History is all the remains that have come down to us from the past, studied with all the critical and interpretative power that the present can bring to the task.* From time to time great masters bring their investigations to fruit in books. To us these serve as the latest words, the best results of the most recent efforts of society to understand itself—but they are not the final words. To the historian the materials for his work are found in all that remains from the ages gone by—in papers, roads, mounds, customs, languages; in monuments, coins, medals, names, titles, inscriptions, charters; in contemporary annals and chronicles; and, finally, in the secondary sources, or histories in the common acceptance of the term. Wherever there remains a chipped flint, a spearhead, a piece of pottery, a pyramid, a picture, a poem, a coliseum, or a coin, there is history.

Says Taine: "What is your first remark on turning over the great stiff leaves of a folio, the yellow sheets of a manuscript, a poem, a code of laws, a declaration of faith? This, you say, was not created alone. It is but a mold, like a fossil shell, an imprint like one of those shapes embossed in stone by an animal which lived and perished. Under the shell there was an animal, and behind the document there was a man. Why do you study the shell except to represent to yourself the animal? So do you study the document only in order to know the man. The shell and the document are lifeless wrecks, valuable only as a clue to the entire and living existence. We must reach back to this existence, endeavor to recreate it."

But observe that when a man writes a narration of the past he writes with all his limitations as regards ability to test the real value of his sources, and ability rightly to interpret them. Does he make use of a chronicle? First he must determine whether it is genuine; then whether it was contemporary, or at what period was written; then what opportunities its author had to know the truth; then what were his personal traits; was he likely to see clearly, to relate impartially? If not, what was his bias, what his limitations? Next comes the harder task—to interpret the significance of events; causes must be understood, results seen. Local affairs must be described in relation to affairs of the world—all must be told with just selection, emphasis, perspective; with that historical imagination and sympathy that does not judge the past by the canons of the present, nor read into it the ideas of the present. Above all the historian must have a passion for truth above that for any party or idea. Such are some of the difficulties that lie in the way of our science. When, moreover, we consider that each man is conditioned by the age in which he lives and must perforce write with limitations and prepossessions, I think we shall all agree that no historian can say the ultimate word.

Another thought that follows as a corollary from our definition is that in history there is a unity and a continuity. Strictly speaking, there is no gap between ancient, medieval, and modern history. Strictly speaking, there are no such divisions. Baron Bunsen dates modern history from the migration of Abraham. Bluntschli makes it begin with Frederick the Great. The truth is, as Freeman has shown, that the age of Pericles or the age of Augustus has more in common with modern times than has the age of Alfred or of Charlemagne. There is another test than that of chronology; namely, stages of growth. In the past of the European world peoples have grown from families into states, from peasantry into the complexity of great city life, from animism into monotheism, from mythology into philosophy; and have yielded place again to primitive peoples who in turn have passed through stages like these and yielded to new nations. Each nation has bequeathed something to its successor; no age has suffered the highest content of the past to be lost entirely. By unconscious inheritance and by conscious striving after the past as part of the present, history has acquired continuity. Freeman's statement that into Rome flowed all the ancient world and out of Rome came the modern world is as true as it is impressive. In a strict sense imperial Rome never died. You may find the eternal city still living in the Kaiser and the Czar, in the language of the Romance peoples, in the codes of European states, in the eagles of their coats of arms, in every college where the classics are read, in a thousand political institutions.

Even here in young America old Rome still lives. When the inaugural procession passes toward the Senate chamber, and the president's address outlines the policy he proposes to pursue, there is Rome! You may find her in the code of Louisiana, in the French and Spanish portions of our history, in the idea of checks and balances in our constitution. Clearest of all, Rome may be seen in the titles, government, and ceremonials of the Roman Catholic Church; for when the caesar passed away, his scepter fell to that new Pontiflex Maximus, the Pope, and to that new Augustus, the Holy Roman emperor of the Middle Ages, an empire which in name at least continued till those heroic times when a new Imperator recalled the days of the great Julius, and sent the eagles of France to proclaim that Napoleon was king over kings.

So it is true in fact, as we should presume a priori, that in history there are only artificial divisions. Society is an organism, ever growing. History is the self-consciousness of this organism. "The roots of the present lie deep in the past." There is no break. But not only is it true that no country can be understood without taking account of all the past; it is also true that we cannot select a stretch of land and say we will limit our study to this land; for local history can only be understood in the light of the history of the world. There is unity as well as continuity. To know the history of contemporary Italy we must know the history of contemporary France, of contemporary Germany. Each acts on each. Ideas, commodities even, refuse the bounds of a nation. All are inextricably connected, so that each is needed to explain the others. This is true especially of our modern world with its complex commerce and means of intellectual connection. In history, then, there is unity and continuity. Each age must be studied in the light of all the past; local history must be viewed in the light of world history.

Now, I think, we are in a position to consider the utility of historical studies. I will not dwell on the dignity of history considered as the self-consciousness of humanity; nor on the mental growth that comes from such a discipline; nor on the vastness of the field; all these occur to you, and their importance will impress you increasingly as you consider history from this point of view. To enable us to behold our own time and place as a part of the stupendous progress of the ages; to see primitive man; to recognize in our midst the undying ideas of Greece; to find Rome's majesty and power alive in present law and institution, still living in our superstitions and our folklore; to enable us to realize the richness of our inheritance, the possibility of our lives, the grandeur of the present—these are some of the priceless services of history.

But I must conclude my remarks with a few words upon the utility of history as affording a training for good citizenship. Doubtless good citizenship is the end for which the public schools exist. Were it otherwise there might be difficulty in justifying the support of them at public expense. The direct and important utility of the study of history in the achievement of this end hardly needs argument.

In the union of public service and historical study Germany has been pre-eminent. For certain governmental positions in that country a university training in historical studies is essential. Ex-President Andrew D. White affirms that a main cause of the efficiency of German administration is the training that officials get from the university study of history and politics. In Paris there is the famous School of Political Sciences which fits men for the public service of France. In the decade closing with 1887 competitive examinations showed the advantages of this training. Of sixty candidates appointed to the council of state, forty were graduates of this school. Of forty-two appointed to the inspection of finance, thirty-nine were from the school; sixteen of seventeen appointees to the court of claims; and twenty of twenty-six appointees to the department of foreign affairs held diplomas from the School of Political Sciences. In these European countries not merely are the departmental officers required to possess historical training; the list of leading statesmen reveals many names eminent in historical science. I need hardly recall to you the great names of Niebuhr the councilor whose history of Rome gave the impetus to our new science; of Stein, the reconstructor of Germany and the projector of the Monumenta Germanicae, that priceless collection of original sources of medieval history. Read the roll of Germany's great public servants and you will find among them such eminent men as Gneist, the authority on English constitutional history; Bluntschli, the able historian of politics; Von Holst, the historian of our own political development; Knies, Roscher, and Wagner, the economists; and many more. I have given you Droysen's conception of history. But Droysen was not simply a historian; he belonged, with the famous historians Treitschke, Mommsen, Von Sybel, to what Lord Acton calls "that central band of writers and statesmen and soldiers who turned the tide that had run for six hundred years, and conquered the centrifugal forces that had reigned in Germany longer than the commons have sat at Westminster."

Nor does England fail to recognize the value of the union of history and politics, as is exemplified by such men as Macaulay, Dilke, Morley, and Bryce, all of whom have been eminent members of Parliament as well as distinguished historical writers. From France and Italy such illustrations could easily be multiplied.

When we turn to America and ask what marriages have occurred between history and statesmanship, we are filled with astonishment at the contrast. It is true that our country has tried to reward literary men; Motley, Irving, Bancroft, Lowell held official positions, but these positions were in the diplomatic service. The "literary fellow"was good enough for Europe. The state gave these men aid rather than called their services to its aid. To this statement I know of but one important exception—George Bancroft. In America statesmanship has been considered something of spontaneous generation, a miraculous birth from our republican institutions. To demand of the statesmen who debate such topics as the tariff, European and South American relations, immigration, labor and railroad problems, a scientific acquaintance with historical politics or economics would be to expose one's self to ridicule in the eyes of the public. I have said that the tribal stage of society demands tribal history and tribal politics.

When a society is isolated it looks with contempt upon the history and institutions of the rest of the world. We shall not be altogether wrong if we say that such tribal ideas concerning our institutions and society have prevailed for many years in this country. Lately historians have turned to the comparative and historical study of our political institutions. The actual working of our constitution as contrasted with the literary theory of it has engaged the attention of able young men. Foreigners like Von Holst and Bryce have shown us a mirror of our political life in the light of the political life of other peoples. Little of this influence has yet attracted the attention of our public men. Count the roll in Senate and House, cabinet and diplomatic service—to say nothing of the state governments—and where are the names famous in history and politics? It is shallow to express satisfaction with this condition and to sneer at "literary fellows." To me it seems that we are approaching a pivotal point in our country's history.

In an earlier part of my remarks I quoted from Thorold Rogers to show how the Turkish conquest of far-off Egypt brought ruin to homes in Antwerp and Bruges. If this was true in that early day, when commercial threads were infinitely less complex than they are now, how profoundly is our present life interlocked with the events of all the world? Heretofore America has remained aloof from the Old World affairs. Under the influence of a wise policy she has avoided political relations with other powers. But it is one of the profoundest lessons that history has to teach, that political relations, in a highly developed civilization, are inextricably connected with economic relations. Already there are signs of a relaxation of our policy of commercial isolation. Reciprocity is a word that meets with increasing favor from all parties. But once fully afloat on the sea of worldwide economic interests, we shall soon develop political interests. Our fishery disputes furnish one example; our Samoan interests another; our Congo relations a third. But perhaps most important are our present and future relations with South America, coupled with our Monroe Doctrine.

It is a settled maxim of international law that the government of a foreign state whose subjects have lent money to another state may interfere to protect the rights of the bondholder, if they are endangered by the borrowing state. As Professor H. B. Adams has pointed out, South American states have close financial relations with many European money-lenders; they are also prone to revolutions. Suppose, now, that England, finding the interests of her bondholders in jeopardy, should step in to manage the affairs of some South American country as she has those of Egypt for the same reasons. Would the United States abandon its popular interpretation of the Monroe Doctrine, or would she give up her policy of noninterference in the political affairs of the outer world? Or suppose our own bondholders in New York, say, to be in danger of loss from revolution in South America—and our increasing tendency to close connection with South American affairs makes this a supposable case—would our government stand idly by while her citizens' interests were sacrificed? Take another case, the protectorate of the proposed interoceanic canal. England will not be content to allow the control of this to rest solely in our hands. Will the United States form an alliance with England for the purpose of this protection? Such questions as these indicate that we are drifting out into European political relations, and that a new statesmanship is demanded, a statesmanship that shall clearly understand European history and present relations, which depend on history.

Again, consider the problems of socialism brought to our shores by European immigrants. We shall never deal rightly with such problems until we understand the historical conditions under which they grew. Thus we meet Europe not only outside our borders but in our very midst. The problem of immigration furnishes many examples of the need of historical study. Consider how our vast Western domain has been settled. Louis XIV devastates the Palatinate, and soon hundreds of its inhabitants are hewing down the forests of Pennsylvania. The bishop of Salzburg persecutes his Protestant subjects, and the woods of Georgia sound to the crack of Teutonic rifles. Presbyterians are oppressed in Ireland, and soon in Tennessee and Kentucky the fires of pioneers gleam. These were but advance guards of the mighty army that has poured into our midst ever since. Every economic change, every political change, every military conscription, every socialistic agitation in Europe, has sent us groups of colonists who have passed out onto our prairies to form new self-governing communities, or who have entered the life of our great cities. These men have come to us historical products, they have brought to us not merely so much bone and sinew, not merely so much money, not merely so much manual skill, they have brought with them deeply inrooted customs and ideas. They are important factors in the political and economic life of the nation. Our destiny is interwoven with theirs; how shall we understand American history without understanding European history? The story of the peopling of America has not yet been written. We do not understand ourselves.

One of the most fruitful fields of study in our country has been the process of growth of our own institutions, local and national. The town and the county, the germs of our political institutions, have been traced back to old Teutonic roots. Gladstone's remark that "the American constitution is the most wonderful work ever struck off at a given time by the brain and purpose of man" has been shown to be misleading, for the constitution was, with all the constructive powers of the fathers, still a growth; and our history is only to be understood as a growth from European history under the new conditions of the New World.

Says Dr. H. B. Adams: "American local history should be studied as a contribution to national history. This country will yet be viewed and reviewed as an organism of historic growth, developing from minute germs, from the very protoplasm of state-life. And some day this country will be studied in its international relations, as an organic part of a larger organism now vaguely called the World-State, but as surely developing through the operation of economic, legal, social, and scientific force as the American Union, the German and British empires are evolving into higher forms. . . .The local consciousness must be expanded into a fuller sense of its historic worth and dignity. We must understand the cosmopolitan relations of modern local life, and its own wholesome conservative power in these days of growing centralization."

If any added argument were needed to show that good citizenship demands the careful study of history, it is in the examples and lessons that the history of other peoples has for us. It is profoundly true that each people makes its own history in accordance with its past. It is true that a purely artificial piece of legislation, unrelated to present and past conditions, is the most short-lived of things. Yet it is to be remembered that it was history that taught us this truth, and that there is, within the limits of the constructive action possible to a state, large scope for the use of this experience of foreign peoples.

I have aimed to offer, then, these considerations: History, I have said, is to be taken in no narrow sense. It is more than past literature, more than past politics, more than past economics. It is the self-consciousness of humanity—humanity's effort to understand itself through the study of its past. Therefore it is not confined to books; the subject is to be studied, not books simply. History has a unity and a continuity; the present needs the past to explain it; and local history must be read as a part of world history. The study has a utility as a mental discipline, and as expanding our ideas regarding the dignity of the present. But perhaps its most practical utility to us, as public school teachers, is its service in fostering good citizenship.

The ideals presented may at first be discouraging. Even to him who devotes his life to the study of history the ideal conception is impossible of attainment. He must select some field and till that thoroughly, be absolute master of it; for the rest he must seek the aid of others whose lives have been given in the true scientific spirit to the study of special fields. The public school teacher must do the best with the libraries at his disposal. We teachers must use all the resources we can obtain and not pin our faith to a single book; we must make history living instead of allowing it to seem mere literature, a mere narration of events that might have occurred on the moon. We must teach the history of a few countries thoroughly, rather than that of many countries superficially. The popularizing of scientific knowledge is one of the best achievements of this age of book-making. It is typical of that social impulse which has led university men to bring the fruits of their study home to the people. In England the social impulse has led to what is known as the university extension movement. University men have left their traditional cloister and gone to live among the working classes, in order to bring to them a new intellectual life. Chautauqua, in our own country, has begun to pass beyond the period of superficial work to a real union of the scientific and the popular. In their summer school they offer courses in American history. Our own state university carries on extensive work in various lines. I believe that this movement in the direction of popularizing historical and scientific knowledge will work a real revolution in our towns and villages as well as in our great cities.

The school teacher is called to do a work above and beyond the instruction in his school. He is called upon to be the apostle of the higher culture to the community in which he is placed. Given a good school or town library—such a one is now within the reach of every hamlet that is properly stimulated to the acquisition of one—and given an energetic, devoted teacher to direct and foster the study of history and politics and economics, we would have an intellectual regeneration of the state. Historical study has for its end to let the community see itself in the light of the past, to give it new thoughts and feelings, new aspirations and energies. Thought and feelings flow into deeds. Here is the motive power that lies behind institutions. This is therefore one of the ways to create good politics; here we can touch the very "age and body of the time, its form and pressure." Have you a thought of better things, a reform to accomplish? "Put it in the air," says the great teacher. Ideas have ruled, will rule. We must make university extension into state life felt in this country as did Germany. Of one thing beware. Avoid as the very unpardonable sin any one-sidedness, any partisan, any partial treatment of history. Do not misinterpret the past for the sake of the present. The man who enters the temple of history must respond devoutly to that invocation of the church, *Sursum corda,* lift up your hearts. No looking at history as an idle tale, a compend of anecdotes; no servile devotion to a textbook; no carelessness of truth about the dead that can no longer speak must be permitted in its sanctuary. "History," says Droysen, "is not the truth and the light; but a striving for it, a sermon on it, a consecration to it."

Bibliographical Note

In the preparation of this lecture free use has been made of the following sources: notes on the lectures of Professor Herbert B. Adams of Johns Hopkins University; J. Cotter Morrison, "History," in the *Encyclopædia Britannica;* Augustine Birrell, "The Muse of History," in the *Contemporary Review* (London), 47:770–80 (June, 1885); Edward A. Freeman, *Methods of Historical Study* (London, 1886); John R. Seeley, "History and Politics," in *Macmillan's Magazine* (New York), 40:289–99, 369–78, 449–58 (August–October, 1879), and "On History Again," 47:67 (November, 1882); Charles K. Adams, *Manual of Historical Literature* (New York, 1889), Preface; Elisha B. Andrews, *Brief Institutes of General History* (3d edition, Boston, 1891), ch. 1; Lord Acton, "German Schools of History," in the *English Historical Review* (London and New York), 1:7–42 (January, 1886); Ernst Bernheim, *Lehrbuch der historischen Methode* (Leipzig, 1889) and *Geschichtsforschung und Geschichtsphilosophie* (Göttingen, 1880); Wilhelm Maurenbrecher, *Uber Methode und Aufgabe der historischen Forschung* (Bonn, 1868) and *Geschichte und Politik* (Leipzig, 1884); Ottokar Lorenz, *Die Geschichtswissenschaft in Hauptrichtungen und Aufgaben* (Berlin, 1886); R.Rocholl, *Die Philosophie der Geschichte* (2 vols., Gottingen, 1878, 1893); and Johann G. Droysen, *Grundriss der Historik* (2nd edition, Leipzig, 1875).

The Significance of the Frontier in American History [1]

In a recent bulletin of the superintendent of the census for 1890 appear these significant words: "Up to and including 1880 the country had a frontier of settlement, but at present the unsettled area has been so broken into by isolated bodies of settlement that there can hardly be said to be a frontier line. In the discussion of its extent, its westward movement, etc., it cannot, therefore, any longer have a place in the census reports."[2] This brief official statement marks the closing of a great historic movement. Up to our own day American history has been in a large degree the history of the colonization of the Great West. The existence of an area of free land, its continuous recession, and the advance of American settlement westward, explain American development. Behind institutions, behind constitutional forms and modifications, lie the vital forces that call these organs into life, and shape them to meet changing conditions. Now, the peculiarity of American institutions is the fact that they have been compelled to adapt themselves to the changes of an expanding people—to the changes involved in crossing a continent, in winning a wilderness, and in developing at each area of this progress out of the primitive economic and political conditions of the frontier into the complexity of city life. Said Calhoun in 1817, "We are great, and rapidly—I was about to say fearfully—growing!"[3] So saying, he touched the distinguishing feature of American life. All peoples show development: the germ theory of politics has *um... actually, there were people there?*

been sufficiently emphasized. In the case of most nations, however, the development has occurred in a limited area; and if the nation has expanded, it has met other growing peoples whom it has conquered. But in the case of the United States we have a different phenomenon. Limiting our attention to the Atlantic coast, we have the familiar phenomenon of the evolution of institutions in a limited area, such as the rise of representative government; the differentiation of simple colonial governments into complex organs; the progress from primitive industrial society, without division of labor, up to manufacturing civilization. But we have in addition to this *a recurrence of the process of evolution in each western area reached in the process of expansion.* Thus American development has exhibited not merely advance along a single line, but a return to primitive conditions on a continually advancing frontier line, and a new development for that area. American social development has been continually beginning over again on the frontier. This perennial rebirth, this fluidity of American life, this expansion westward with its new opportunities, its continuous touch with the simplicity of primitive society, furnish the forces dominating American character. The true point of view in the history of this nation is not the Atlantic coast, it is the Great West. Even the slavery struggle, which is made so exclusive an object of attention by writers like Professor Von Holst, occupies its important place in American history because of its relation to westward expansion.

In this advance, the frontier is the outer edge of the wave—the meeting point between savagery and civilization. Much has been written about the frontier from the point of view of border warfare and the chase, but as a field for the serious study of the economist and the historian it has been neglected.

What is the frontier? It is not the European frontier—a fortified boundary line running through dense populations. The most significant thing about it is, that it lies at the hither edge of free land. In the census reports it is treated as the margin of that settlement which has a density of two or more to the square mile. The term is an elastic one, and for our purpose does not need sharp definition. We shall consider the whole frontier belt, including the Indian country and the outer margin of the "settled areas" of the census reports. This paper will make no attempt to treat the subject exhaustively; its aim is simply to call attention to the frontier as a fertile field for investigation, and to suggest some of the problems which arise in connection with it.

In the settlement of America we have to observe how European life entered the continent, and how America modified and developed that life, and reacted on Europe. Our early history is the study of European germs developing in an American environment. Too exclusive attention has been paid by institutional students to the Germanic origins, too little to the American factors. Now, the frontier is the line of most rapid and effective Americanization. The wilderness masters the colonist. It finds him a European in dress, industries, tools, modes of travel, and thought. It takes him from the railroad car and puts him in the birch canoe. It strips off the garments of civilization, and arrays him in the hunting shirt and the moccasin. It puts him in the log cabin of the Cherokee and the Iroquois, and runs an Indian palisade around him. Before long he has gone to planting Indian corn and plowing with a sharp stick; he shouts the war cry and takes the scalp in orthodox Indian fashion. In short, at the frontier the environment is at first too strong for the man. He must accept the conditions which it furnishes, or perish, and so he fits himself into the Indian clearings and follows the Indian trails. Little by little he transforms the wilderness, but the outcome is not the old Europe, not simply the development of Germanic germs, any more than the first phenomenon was a case of reversion to the Germanic mark. The fact is, that here is a new product that is American. At first, the frontier was the Atlantic coast. It was the frontier of Europe in a very real sense. Moving westward, the frontier became more and more American. *As successive terminal moraines result from successive glaciations, so each frontier leaves its traces behind it, and when it becomes a settled area the region still partakes of the frontier*

Frontier the most American part of America .

characteristics. Thus the advance of the frontier has meant a steady movement away from the influence of Europe, a steady growth of independence on American lines. And to study this advance, the men who grew up under these conditions, and the political, economic and social results of it, is to study the really American part of our history.

Stages of Frontier Advance

In the course of the seventeenth century the frontier was advanced up the Atlantic river courses, just beyond the "fall line," and the tidewater region became the settled area. In the first half of the eighteenth century another advance occurred. Traders followed the Delaware and Shawnese Indians to the Ohio as early as the end of the first quarter of the century.[4] Gov. Spottswood, of Virginia, made an expedition in 1714 across the Blue Ridge. The end of the first quarter of the century saw the advance of the Scotch-Irish and the Palatine Germans up the Shenandoah Valley into the western part of Virginia, and along the Piedmont region of the Carolinas.[5] The Germans in New York pushed the frontier of settlement up the Mohawk to German Flats.[6] In Pennsylvania the town of Bedford indicates the line of settlement. Settlements had begun on New River, a branch of the Kanawha, and on the sources of the Yadkin and French Broad.[7] The king attempted to arrest the advance by his proclamation of 1763,[8] forbidding settlements beyond the sources of the rivers flowing into the Atlantic; but in vain. In the period of the Revolution the frontier crossed the Alleghanies into Kentucky and Tennessee, and the upper waters of the Ohio were settled.[9] When the first census was taken in 1790, the continuous settled area was bounded by a line which ran near the coast of Maine, and included New England except a portion of Vermont and New Hampshire, New York along the Hudson and up the Mohawk about Schenectady, eastern and southern Pennsylvania, Virginia well across the Shenandoah Valley, and the Carolinas and eastern Georgia.[10] Beyond this region of continuous settlement were the small settled areas of Kentucky and Tennessee and the Ohio, with the mountains intervening between them and the Atlantic area, thus giving a new and important character to the frontier. The isolation of the region increased its peculiarly American tendencies, and the need of transportation facilities to connect it with the East called out important schemes of internal improvement, which will be noted farther on. The "West," as a self- conscious section, began to evolve.

From decade to decade distinct advances of the frontier occurred. By the census of 1820[11] the settled area included Ohio, southern Indiana and Illinois, southeastern Missouri, and about one-half of Louisiana. This settled area had surrounded Indian areas, and the management of these tribes became an object of political concern. The frontier region of the time lay along the Great Lakes, where Astor's American Fur Company operated in the Indian trade,[12] and beyond the Mississippi, where Indian traders extended their activity even to the Rocky Mountains; Florida also furnished frontier conditions. The Mississippi river region was the scene of typical frontier settlements.[13]

The rising steam navigation[14] on western waters, the opening of the Erie canal, and the westward extension of cotton culture[15] added five frontier states to the Union in this period. Grund, writing in 1836, declares: "It appears then that the universal disposition of Americans to emigrate to the western wilderness, in order to enlarge their dominion over inanimate nature, is the actual result of an expansive power which is inherent in them, and which by continually agitating all classes of society is constantly throwing a large portion of the whole population on the extreme confines of the state, in order to gain space for its development. Hardly is a new state or territory formed before the same principle manifests itself again and gives rise to a further emigration; and so is it destined to go on until a physical barrier must finally obstruct its progress."[16]

In the middle of this century the line indicated by the present eastern boundary of Indian Territory, Nebraska, and Kansas, marked the frontier of the Indian country.[17] Minnesota and Wisconsin still exhibited frontier conditions,[18] but the distinctive frontier of the period is found in California, where the gold discoveries had sent a sudden tide of adventurous miners, and in Oregon, and the settlements in Utah.[19] As the frontier had leaped over the Alleghanies, so now it skipped the Great Plains and the Rocky Mountains; and in the same way that the advance of the frontiersmen beyond the Alleghanies had caused the rise of important questions of transportation and internal improvement, so now the settlers beyond the Rocky Mountains needed means of communication with the East, and in the furnishing of these, arose the settlement of the Great Plains, and the development of still another kind of frontier life. Railroads, fostered by land grants, sent an increasing tide of immigrants into the far West. The United States army fought a series of Indian wars in Minnesota, Dakota, and the Indian Territory.

By 1880, the settled area had been pushed into northern Michigan, Wisconsin, and Minnesota, along Dakota rivers, and in the Black Hills region, and was ascending the rivers of Kansas and Nebraska. The development of mines in Colorado had drawn isolated frontier settlements into that region, and Montana and Idaho were receiving settlers. The frontier was found in these mining camps and the ranches of the great plains. The superintendent of the census for 1890 reports, as previously stated, that the settlements of the West lie so scattered over the region that there can no longer be said to be a frontier line.

In these successive frontiers we find natural boundary lines which have served to mark and to affect the characteristics of the frontiers, namely: The "fall line;" the Alleghany Mountains; the Mississippi; the Missouri where its direction approximates north and south; the line of the arid lands, approximately the 99th meridian; and the Rocky Mountains. The fall line marked the frontier of the seventeenth century; the Alleghanies that of the eigh-

↓

teenth; the Mississippi that of the first quarter of the nineteenth; the Missouri that of the middle of this century (omitting the California movement); and the belt of the Rocky Mountains and the arid tract, the present frontier. Each was won by a series of Indian Wars.

The Frontier Furnishes a Field for
Comparative Study of Social Development

Frontiers a succession —

At the Atlantic frontier one can study the germs of processes repeated at each successive frontier. We have the complex European life, sharply precipitated by the wilderness into the simplicity of primitive conditions. The first frontier had to meet its Indian question, its question of the disposition of the public domain, of the means of intercourse with the older settlements, of the extension of political organization, of religious and educational activity. And the settlement of these and similar questions for one frontier served as a guide for the next. The American student needs not to go to the "prim little townships of Sleswick" for illustrations of the law of continuity and development. For example, he may study the origin of our land policies in the colonial land policy; he may see how the system grew by adapting the statutes to the customs of the successive frontiers.[20] He may see how the mining experience in the lead region of Wisconsin, Illinois, and Iowa was applied to the mining laws of the Rockies,[21] and how our Indian policy has been a series of experimentations on successive frontiers. Each tier of new states has found, in the older ones, material for its constitutions.[23] Each frontier has made similar contributions to American character, as will be discussed farther on.

stages in Am development

But with all these similarities there are essential differences due to the place element and the time element. It is evident that the farming frontier of the Mississippi Valley presents different conditions from the mining frontier of the Rocky Mountains. The frontier reached by the Pacific railroad, surveyed into rectangles, guarded by the United States army, and recruited by the daily immigrant ship, moves forward at a swifter pace and in a different way than the frontier reached by the birch canoe or the pack horse. The geologist traces patiently the shores of ancient seas, maps their areas, and compares the older and the newer. It would be a work worth the historian's labors to mark these various frontiers and in detail compare one with another. Not only would there result a more adequate conception of American development and characteristics, but invaluable additions would be made to the history of society.

Loria,[23] the Italian economist, has urged the study of colonial life as an aid in understanding the stages of European development, affirming that colonial settlement is for economic science what the mountain is for geology, bringing to light primitive stratifications. "America," he says, "has the key to the historical enigma which Europe has sought for centuries in vain, and the land which has no history reveals luminously the course of universal history." He is right. The United States lies like a huge page in the history of society. Line by line as we read from west to east we find the record of social evolution. It begins with the Indian and the hunter; it goes on to tell of the disintegration of savagery by the entrance of the trader, the path-finder of civilization; we read the annals of the pastoral stage in ranch life; the exploitation of the soil by the raising of unrotated crops of corn and wheat in sparsely settled farming communities; the intensive culture of the denser farm settlement; and finally the manufacturing organization with city and factory system.[24] This page is familiar to the student of census statistics, but how little of it has been used by our historians. Each of these areas has had an influence in our economic and political history; the evolution of each into a higher stage has worked political transformations. But what constitutional historian has made any adequate attempt to interpret political facts by the light of these social areas and changes?

The Atlantic frontier was compounded of fisherman, fur

trader, miner, cattle raiser, and farmer. Excepting the fisherman, each type of industry was on the march toward the West, impelled by an irresistible attraction. Each passed in successive waves across the continent. Stand at Cumberland Gap and watch the procession of civilization, marching single file—the buffalo, following the trail to the salt springs, the Indian, the fur trader and hunter, the cattle raiser, the pioneer farmer—and the frontier has passed by. Stand at South Pass in the Rockies a century later, and see the same procession with wider intervals between. The unequal rate of advance compels us to distinguish the frontier into the trader's frontier, the rancher's frontier, or the miner's frontier, and the farmer's frontier. When the mines and the cowpens were still near the fall line the traders' pack trains were tinkling across the Alleghanies, and the French on the Great Lakes were fortifying their posts, alarmed by the British trader's birch canoe. When the trappers scaled the Rockies, the farmer was still near the mouth of the Missouri.

The Indian Trader's Frontier

Why was it that the Indian trader passed so rapidly across the continent? What effects followed from the trader's frontier? The trade was coeval with American discovery. The Norsemen, Vespuccius, Verrazani, Hudson, John Smith, all trafficked for furs. The Plymouth pilgrims settled in Indian cornfields, and their first return cargo was of beaver and lumber. The records of the various New England colonies show how steadily exploration was carried into the wilderness by this trade. What is true for New England is, as would be expected, even plainer for the rest of the colonies. All along the coast from Maine to Georgia the Indian trade opened up the river courses. Steadily the trader passed westward, utilizing the older lines of French trade. The Ohio, the Great Lakes, the Mississippi, the Missouri and the Platte, the lines of western advance, were ascended by traders.

They found the passes in the Rocky Mountains and guided Lewis and Clark,[25] Fremont, and Bidwell. The explanation of the rapidity of this advance is bound up with the effects of the trader on the Indian. The trading post left the unarmed tribes at the mercy of those that had purchased fire-arms—a truth which the Iroquois Indians wrote in blood, and so the remote and unvisited tribes gave eager welcome to the trader. "The savages," wrote LaSalle, "take better care of us French than of their own children; from us only can they get guns and goods." This accounts for the trader's power and the rapidity of his advance. Thus the disintegrating forces of civilization entered the wilderness. Every river valley and Indian trail became a fissure in Indian society, and so that society became honeycombed. Long before the pioneer farmer appeared on the scene, primitive Indian life had passed away. The farmers met Indians armed with guns. The trading frontier, while steadily undermining Indian power by making the tribes ultimately dependent on the whites, yet, through its sale of guns, gave to the Indians increased power of resistance to the farming frontier. French colonization was dominated by its trading frontier; English colonization by its farming frontier. There was an antagonism between the two frontiers as between the two nations. Said Duquesne to the Iroquois, "Are you ignorant of the difference between the King of England and the King of France? Go see the forts that our king has established and you will see that you can still hunt under their very walls. They have been placed for your advantage in places which you frequent. The English, on the contrary, are no sooner in possession of a place than the game is driven away. The forest falls before them as they advance, and the soil is laid bare so that you can scarce find the wherewithal to erect a shelter for the night."

And yet, in spite of this opposition of the interests of the trader and the farmer, the Indian trade pioneered the way for civilization. The buffalo trail became the Indian trail, and this became the trader's "trace;" the trails widened into roads, and the roads into turnpikes, and these in turn were transformed into railroads.

The same origin can be shown for the railroads of the South, the far West, and the Dominion of Canada. The trading posts reached by these trails were on the sites of Indian villages which had been placed in positions suggested by nature; and these trading posts, situated so as to command the water systems of the country, have grown into such cities as Albany, Pittsburg, Detroit, Chicago, St. Louis, Council Bluffs, and Kansas City. Thus civilization in America has followed the arteries made by geology, pouring an ever richer tide through them, until at last the slender paths of aboriginal intercourse have been broadened and interwoven into the complex mazes of modern commercial lines; the wilderness has been interpenetrated by lines of civilization, growing ever more numerous. It is like the steady growth of a complex nervous system for the originally simple, inert continent. If one would understand why we are today one nation, rather than a collection of isolated states, he must study this economic and social consolidation of the country. In this progress from savage conditions lie topics for the evolutionist.[26]

The effect of the Indian frontier as a consolidating agent in our history is important. From the close of the seventeenth century various intercolonial congresses have been called to treat with Indians and establish common measures of defense. Particularism was strongest in colonies with no Indian frontier. This frontier stretched along the western border like a cord of union. The Indian was a common danger, demanding united action. Most celebrated of these conferences was the Albany congress of 1754, called to treat with the Six Nations, and to consider plans of union. Even a cursory reading of the plan proposed by the congress reveals the importance of the frontier. The powers of the general council and the officers were, chiefly, the determination of peace and war with the Indians, the regulation of Indian trade, the purchase of Indian lands, and the creation and government of new settlements as a security against the Indians. It is evident that the unifying tendencies of the Revolutionary period were facilitated by the previous co-operation in the regulation of the frontier. In this connection may be mentioned the importance of the frontier, from that day to this, as a military training school, keeping alive the power of resistance to aggression, and developing the stalwart and rugged qualities of the frontiersman.

The Rancher's Frontier

It would not be possible in the limits of this paper to trace the other frontiers across the continent. Travellers of the eighteenth century found the "cowpens" among the canebrakes and peavine pastures of the South, and the "cow drivers" took their droves to Charleston, Philadelphia, and New York.[27] Travellers at the close of the War of 1812 met droves of more than a thousand cattle and swine from the interior of Ohio going to Pennsylvania to fatten for the Philadelphia market.[28] The ranges of the Great Plains, with ranch and cowboy and nomadic life, are things of yesterday and of today. The experience of the Carolina cowpens guided the ranchers of Texas. One element favoring the rapid extension of the rancher's frontier is the fact that in a remote country lacking transportation facilities the product must be in small bulk, or must be able to transport itself, and the cattle raiser could easily drive his product to market. The effect of these great ranches on the subsequent agrarian history of the localities in which they existed should be studied.

The Farmer's Frontier

The maps of the census reports show an uneven advance of the farmer's frontier, with tongues of settlement pushed forward and with indentations of wilderness. In part this is due to Indian resistance, in part to the location of river valleys and passes, in part to the unequal force of the centers of frontier attraction. Among the important centers of attraction may be mentioned the following: fertile and favorably situated soils, salt springs, mines, and army posts.

Army Posts

The frontier army post, serving to protect the settlers from the Indians, has also acted as a wedge to open the Indian country, and has been a nucleus for settlement.[29] In this connection mention should also be made of the government military and exploring expeditions in determining the lines of settlement. But all the more important expeditions were greatly indebted to the earliest pathmakers, the Indian guides, the traders and trappers, and the French voyageurs, who were inevitable parts of governmental expeditions from the days of Lewis and Clark.[30] Each expedition was an epitome of the previous factors in western advance.

Salt Springs

In an interesting monograph, Victor Hehn[31] has traced the effect of salt upon early European development, and has pointed out how it affected the lines of settlement and the form of administration. A similar study might be made for the salt springs of the United States. The early settlers were tied to the coast by the need of salt, without which they could not preserve their meats or live in comfort. Writing in 1752, Bishop Spangenberg says of a colony for which he was seeking lands in North Carolina, "They will require salt & other necessaries which they can neither manufacture nor raise. Either they must go to Charleston, which is 300 miles distant. . . . Or else they must go to Boling's Point in Vᵃ on a branch of the James & is also 300 miles from here . . . Or else they must go down the Roanoke—I know not how many miles— where salt is brought up from the Cape Fear."[32] This may serve as a typical illustration. An annual pilgrimage to the coast for salt thus became essential. Taking flocks or furs and ginseng root, the early settlers sent their pack trains after seeding time each year to the coast.[33] This proved to be an important educational influence, since it was almost the only way in which the pioneer learned what was going on in the East. But when discovery was made of the salt springs of the Kanawha, and the Holston, and Kentucky, and central New York, the West began to be freed from dependence on the coast. It was in part the effect of finding these salt springs that enabled settlement to cross the mountains.

From the time the mountains rose between the pioneer and the seaboard, a new order of Americanism arose. The West and the East began to get out of touch of each other. The settlements from the sea to the mountains kept connection with the rear and had a certain solidarity. But the overmountain men grew more and more independent. The East took a narrow view of American advance, and nearly lost these men. Kentucky and Tennessee history bears abundant witness to the truth of this statement. The East began to try to hedge and limit westward expansion. Though Webster could declare that there were no Alleghanies in his politics, yet in politics in general they were a very solid factor.

Land

Good soils have been the most continuous attraction to the farmer's frontier. The land hunger of the Virginians drew them down the rivers into Carolina, in early colonial days; the search for soils took the Massachusetts men to Pennsylvania and to New York. The exploitation of the beasts took hunter and trader to the west, the exploitation of the grasses took the rancher west, and the exploitation of the virgin soil of the river valleys and prairies attracted the farmer. As the eastern lands were taken up migration flowed across them to the west. Daniel Boone, the great backwoodsman, who combined the occupations of hunter, trader, cattle raiser, farmer and surveyor—learning, probably from the traders, of the fertility of the lands on the upper Yadkin, where the traders were wont to rest as they took their way to the Indians, left his Pennsylvania home with his father, and passed down the Great Valley road to that stream. Learning from a trader whose posts were on the Red River in Kentucky of its game and rich pastures, he pioneered the way for farmers to that region. Thence he passed to the frontier of Missouri, where his settlement was long a landmark on the frontier. Here again he helped to open the way for civilization, finding salt licks, and trails, and land. His son was among the earliest trappers in the passes of the Rocky Mountains, and his party are said to have been the first to camp on the present site of Denver. His grandson, Col. A. J. Boone, of Colorado, was a power among the Indians of the Rocky Mountains, and was appointed an agent by the government. Kit Carson's mother was a Boone.[34] Thus this family epitomises the backwoodsman's advance across the continent.

The farmer's advance came in a distinct series of waves. In Peck's *New Guide to the West,* published in Cincinnati in 1848, occurs this suggestive passage:

"Generally, in all the western settlements, three classes, like the waves of the ocean, have rolled one after the other. First, comes the pioneer, who depends for the subsistence of his family chiefly upon the natural growth of vegetation, called the 'range,' and the proceeds of hunting. His implements of agriculture are rude, chiefly of his own make, and his efforts directed mainly to a crop of corn and a 'truck patch.' The last is a rude garden for growing cabbage, beans, corn for roasting ears, cucumbers and potatoes. A log cabin, and, occasionally, a stable and corn-crib, and a field of a dozen acres, the timber girdled or 'deadened,' and fenced, are enough for his occupancy. It is quite immaterial whether he ever becomes the owner of the soil. He is the occupant for the time being, pays no rent, and feels as independent as the 'lord of the manor.' With a horse, cow, and one or two breeders of swine, he strikes into the woods with his family, and becomes the founder of a new county, or perhaps state. He builds his cabin, gathers around him a few other families of similar tastes and habits, and occupies till the range is somewhat subdued, and hunting a little precarious, or, which is more frequently the case, till neighbors crowd around, roads, bridges, and fields annoy him, and he lacks elbow room. The pre-emption law enables him to dispose of his cabin and corn-field to the next class of emigrants; and, to employ his own figures, he 'breaks for the high timber,' 'clears out for the New Purchase,' or migrates to Arkansas or Texas, to work the same process over.

"The next class of emigrants purchase the lands, add field to field, clear out the roads, throw rough bridges over the streams, put up hewn log houses, with glass windows and brick or stone chimneys, occasionally plant orchards, build mills, school-houses, court-houses, etc., and exhibit the picture and forms of plain, frugal, civilized life.

"Another wave rolls on. The men of capital and enterprise come. The settler is ready to sell out, and take the advantage of the rise in property—push farther into the interior and become, himself, a man of capital and enterprise in turn. The small village rises to a spacious town or city; substantial edifices of brick, extensive fields, orchards, gardens, colleges and churches are seen. Broadcloths, silks, leghorns, crapes, and all the refinements, luxuries, elegancies, frivolities and fashions are in vogue. Thus wave after wave is rolling westward—the real *Eldorado* is still farther on.

"A portion of the two first classes remain stationary amidst the general movement, improve their habits and condition, and rise in the scale of society.

"The writer has traveled much amongst the first class—the real pioneers. He has lived many years in connection with the second grade; and now the third wave is sweeping over large districts of Indiana, Illinois and Missouri. Migration has become almost a habit in the West. Hundreds of men can be found, not over fifty years of age, who have settled for the fourth, fifth or sixth time on a new spot. To sell out and remove only a few hundred miles makes up a portion of the variety of backwoods life and manners."[25]

Omitting the pioneer farmer who moves from the love of adventure, the advance of the more steady farmer is easy to understand. Obviously the immigrant was attracted by the cheap lands of the frontier, and even the native farmer felt their influence strongly. Year by year the farmers who lived on soil, whose returns were diminished by unrotated crops, were offered the virgin soil of the frontier at nominal prices. Their growing families demanded more lands, and these were dear. The competition of the unexhausted, cheap and easily tilled prairie lands compelled the farmer either to go west and continue the exhaustion of the soil on a new frontier, or to adopt intensive culture. Thus the census of 1890 shows, in the Northwest, many counties in which there is an absolute, or a relative, decrease of population. These states have been sending farmers to advance the frontier on the plains, and have themselves begun to turn to intensive farming and to manufacture. A decade before this, Ohio had shown the same transition stage. Thus the demand for land and the love of wilderness freedom drew the frontier ever onward.

Having now roughly outlined the various kinds of frontiers, and their modes of advance, chiefly from the point of view of the frontier itself, we may next inquire what were the influences on the East and on the Old World. A rapid enumeration of some of the more noteworthy effects is all that I have time for.

Composite Nationality

First, we note that the frontier promoted the formation of a composite nationality for the American people. The coast was preponderantly English, but the later tides of continental immigration flowed across to the free lands. This was the case from the early colonial days. The Scotch Irish and the Palatine Germans, or "Pennsylvania Dutch," furnished the stock of the colonial frontier. With these peoples were also the freed indented servants, or redemptioners, who at the expiration of their time of service passed to the frontier. Governor Spottswood of Virginia writes in 1717, "The inhabitants of our frontiers are composed generally of such as have been transported hither as servants, and, being out of

their time, settle themselves where land is to be taken up and that
will produce the necessarys of life with little labor."[36] Very generally these redemptioners were of non-English stock. In the cru-
cible of the frontier the immigrants were Americanized, liberated
and fused into a mixed race, English in neither nationality or
characteristics. The process has gone on from the early days to our
own. Burke and other writers in the middle of the eighteenth century believed that Pennsylvania[37] was "threatened with the danger of being wholly foreign in language, manners, and perhaps
even inclinations." The Germans and Scotch-Irish elements in
the frontier of the South were only less great. In the middle of the
present century the German element in Wisconsin was already so
considerable that leading publicists looked to the creation of a
German state out of the commonwealth by concentrating their
colonization.[38] Such examples teach us to beware of misinterpret-
ing the fact that there is a common English speech in America
into a belief that the stock is also English.

Industrial Independence

In another way the advance of the frontier decreased our dependence on England. The coast, particularly of the South, lacked
diversified industries, and was dependent on England for the
bulk of its supplies. In the South there was even a dependence on
the Northern colonies for articles of food. Governor Glenn of
South Carolina writes in the middle of the eighteenth century:
"Our trade with New York and Philadelphia was of this sort,
draining us of all the little money and bills we could gather from
other places for their bread, flour, beer, hams, bacon and other
things of their produce, all which, except beer, our new townships
begin to supply us with, which are settled with very industrious
and thriving Germans. This no doubt diminishes the number of
shipping and the appearance of our trade, but it is far from being
a detriment to us."[39] Before long the frontier created a demand for
merchants. As it retreated from the coast it became less and less

possible for England to bring her supplies directly to the consumer's wharfs, and carry away staple crops, and staple crops began to give way to diversified agriculture for a time. The effect of this phase of the frontier action upon the northern section is perceived when we realize how the advance of the frontier aroused seaboard cities like Boston, New York, and Baltimore, to engage in rivalry for what Washington called "the extensive and valuable trade of a rising empire."

Effects on National Legislation

The legislation which most developed the powers of the national government, and played the largest part in its activity, was conditioned on the frontier. Writers have discussed the subjects of tariff, land, and internal improvement, as pendants to the slavery question. But when American history comes to be rightly viewed it will be seen that the slavery question is an incident. In the period from the end of the first half of the present century to the close of the Civil War, slavery rose to primary but far from exclusive importance. But this does not justify Professor Von Holst (to take an example) in treating our constitutional history in its formative period down to 1828 in a single volume, and giving six volumes to the history of slavery from 1828 to 1861, under the title of a *Constitutional History of the United States*. The growth of nationalism and the evolution of American political institutions were dependent on the advance for the frontier. Even so recent a writer as Rhodes, in his *History of the United States since the Compromise of 1850,* has treated the legislation called out by the western advance as incidental to the slavery struggle.

This is a wrong perspective. The pioneer needed the goods of the coast, and so the grand series of internal improvement and railroad legislation began, with potent nationalizing effects. But the West was not content with bringing the farm to the factory. Under the lead of Clay—"Harry of the West"—protective tariffs were passed, with the cry of bringing the factory to the farm.

The Public Domain

The public domain has been a force of profound importance in the nationalization and development of the government. The effects of the struggle of the landed and the landless states, and of the Ordinance of 1787, need no discussion.[40] Administratively the frontier called out some of the highest and most vitalizing activities of the general government. The purchase of Louisiana was perhaps the constitutional turning-point in the history of the republic, inasmuch as it afforded both a new area for national legislation, and the occasion of the downfall of the policy of strict construction. But the purchase of Louisiana was called out by frontier needs and demands. As frontier states accrued to the Union, the national power grew. In a speech on the dedication of the Calhoun monument, Lamar explained: "In 1789 the states were the creators of the federal government; in 1861, the federal government was the creator of a large majority of the states."

When we consider the public domain from the point of view of the sale and disposal of the public lands, we are again brought face to face with the frontier. The policy of the United States in dealing with its lands is in sharp contrast with the European system of scientific administration. Efforts to make this domain a source of revenue, and to withhold it from emigrants in order that settlement might be compact, were in vain. The jealousy and the fears of the East were powerless in the face of the demands of the frontiersmen. John Quincy Adams was obliged to confess: "My own system of administration, which was to make the national domain the inexhaustible fund for progressive and unceasing internal improvement, has failed." The reason is obvious; systems of administration was not what the West demanded; it wanted land. Adams states the situation as follows: "The slave holders of the South have bought the co-operation of the western country by the bribe of the western lands, abandoning to the new western states their own proportion of the public property and aiding them in the design of grasping all the lands into their own hands. Thomas H. Benton was the author of this system, which he brought forward as a substitute for the American system of Mr. Clay and to supplant him as the leading statesman of the West. Mr. Clay, by his tariff compromise with Mr. Calhoun, abandoned his own American system. At the same time he brought forward a plan for distributing among all the states of the Union the proceeds of the sales of the public lands. His bill for that purpose passed both Houses of Congress, but was vetoed by President Jackson, who, in his annual message of December 1832, formally recommended that all public lands should be gratuitously given away to individual adventurers and to the states in which the lands are situated.[41]

"No subject," said Henry Clay, "which has presented itself to the present, or perhaps any preceding, congress, is of greater magnitude than that of the public lands." When we consider the far-reaching effects of the government's land policy upon political, economic, and social aspects of American life, we are disposed to agree with him. But this legislation was framed under frontier influences, and under the lead of Western statesmen like Benton and Jackson. Said Senator Scott of Indiana in 1841: "I consider the pre-emption law merely declaratory of the custom or common law of the settlers."

National Tendencies of the Frontier

It is safe to say that the legislation with regard to land, tariff, and internal improvements—the American system of the nationalizing Whig party—was conditioned on frontier ideas and needs. But it was not merely in legislative action that the frontier worked against the sectionalism of the coast. The economic and social characteristics of the frontier worked against sectionalism. The men of the frontier had closer resemblances to the Middle region than to either of the other sections. Pennsylvania had been the seed-plot of frontier emigration, and, although she passed on her settlers along the Great Valley into the west of Virginia and the Carolinas, yet the industrial society of these Southern frontiersmen was always more like that of the Middle region than like that of the tidewater portion of the South, which later came to spread its industrial type throughout the South.

The Middle region, entered by New York harbor, was an open door to all Europe. The tidewater part of the South represented typical Englishmen, modified by a warm climate and servile labor, and living in baronial fashion on great plantations; New England stood for a special English movement—Puritanism. The Middle region was less English than the other sections. It had a wide mixture of nationalities, a varied society, the mixed town and county system of local government, a varied economic life, many religious sects. In short it was a region mediating between New England and the South, and the East and the West. It represented that composite nationality which the contemporary United States exhibits, that juxtaposition of non-English groups, occupying a valley or a little settlement, and presenting reflections of the map of Europe in their variety. It was democratic and non-sectional, if not national; "easy, tolerant and contented;" rooted strongly in material prosperity. It was typical of the modern United States. It was least sectional, not only because it lay between North and South, but also because with no barriers to shut out its frontiers from its settled region, and with a system of connecting waterways, the Middle region mediated between East and West as well as between North and South. Thus it became the typically American region. Even the New Englander, who was shut out from the frontier by the Middle region, tarrying in New York or Pennsylvania on his westward march, lost the acuteness of his sectionalism on the way.[42]

Until the spread of cotton culture into the interior gave homogeneity to the South, the western part of it showed tendencies to fall away from the faith of the fathers into internal improvement legislation and nationalism. In the Virginia convention of 1829–30, called to revise the constitution, Mr. Leigh, of Chesterfield, one of the tidewater counties, declared:

"One of the main causes of discontent which led to this convention, that which had the strongest influence in overcoming our veneration for the work of our fathers, which taught us to contemn the sentiments of Henry and Mason and Pendleton, which weaned us from our reverence for the constituted authorities of the states, was an overweening passion for internal improvement. I say this with perfect knowledge; for it has been avowed to me by gentlemen from the West over and over again. And let me tell the gentleman from Albemarle (Mr. Gordon) that it has been another principal object of those who set this ball of revolution in motion, to overturn the doctrine of state rights, of which Virginia has been the very pillar, and to remove the barrier she has interposed to the interference of the federal government in that same work of internal improvement by so reorganizing the legislature that Virginia, too, may be hitched to the federal car."

It was this nationalizing tendency of the West that transformed the democracy of Jefferson into the national republicanism of Monroe and the democracy of Andrew Jackson. The West of the War of 1812, the West of Clay, and Benton, and Harrison, and Andrew Jackson, shut off by the Middle states and the mountains from the coast sections, had a solidarity of its own with national tendencies. On the tide of the Father of Waters, North and South met and mingled into a nation. Interstate migration went steadily on—a process of cross-fertilization of ideas and institutions. The fierce struggle of the sections over slavery on the western frontier does not diminish the truth of this statement; it proves the truth of it. Slavery was a sectional trait that would not down, but in the West it could not remain sectional. It was the greatest of frontiersmen who declared: "I believe this government cannot endure permanently half slave and half free. It will become all of one thing, or all of the other." Nothing works for nationalism like inter-

course within the nation. Mobility of population is death to local-
ism, and the western frontier worked irresistibly in unsettling
population. The effects reached back from the frontier and affected profoundly the Atlantic coast, and even the Old World.

Growth of Democracy

But the most important effect of the frontier has been in the
promotion of democracy here and in Europe. As has been pointed
out, the frontier is productive of individualism. Complex society
is precipitated by the wilderness into a kind of primitive organization based on the family. The tendency is anti-social. It pro-
duces antipathy to control, and particularly to any direct control.
The tax-gatherer is viewed as a representative of oppression. Professor Osgood, in an able article,[43] has pointed out that the frontier
conditions prevalent in the colonies are important factors in the
explanation of the American revolution, where individual liberty
was sometimes confused with absence of all effective government.
The same conditions aid in explaining the difficulty of instituting
a strong government in the period of the confederacy. The frontier individualism has from the beginning promoted democracy.

The frontier states that came into the Union in the first quarter
of a century of its existence came in with democratic suffrage pro-
visions, and had reactive effects of the highest importance upon
the older states whose peoples were being attracted there. It was
western New York that forced an extension of suffrage in the constitutional convention of that state in 1820; and it was *western* Virginia that compelled the tidewater region to put a more liberal
suffrage provision in the constitution framed in 1830, and to give
to the frontier region a more nearly proportionate representation
with the tidewater aristocracy. The rise of democracy as an effective force in the nation came in with western preponderance under Jackson and William Henry Harrison, and it meant the triumph of the frontier—with all of its good and with all of its evil

elements.[44] An interesting illustration of the tone of frontier democracy in 1830 comes from the same debates in the Virginia convention already referred to. A representative from western Virginia declared: "But, sir, it is not the increase of population in the West which this gentleman ought to fear. It is the energy which the mountain breeze and western habits impart to those emigrants. They are regenerated, politically I mean, sir. They soon become *working politicians;* and the difference, sir, between a *talking* and a *working* politician is immense. The Old Dominion has long been celebrated for producing great orators; the ablest metaphysicians in policy; men that can split hairs in all abstruse questions of political economy. But at home, or when they return from congress, they have negroes to fan them asleep. But a Pennsylvania, a New York, an Ohio, or a western Virginia statesman, though far inferior in logic, metaphysics and rhetoric to an old Virginia statesman, has this advantage, that when he returns home he takes off his coat and takes hold of the plough. This gives him bone and muscle, sir, and preserves his republican principles pure and uncontaminated."

So long as free land exists, the opportunity for a competency exists, and economic power secures political power. But the democracy born of free land, strong in selfishness and individualism, intolerant of administrative experience and education, and pressing individual liberty beyond its proper bounds, has its dangers as well as its benefits. Individualism in America has allowed a laxity in regard to governmental affairs which has rendered possible the spoils system, and all the manifest evils that follow from the lack of a highly developed civic spirit. In this connection may be noted also the influence of frontier conditions in permitting lax business honor, inflated paper currency and wild-cat banking. The colonial and revolutionary frontier was the region whence emanated many of the worst forms of an evil currency.[45] The West in the War of 1812 repeated the phenomenon on the frontier of that day, while the speculation and wild-cat banking of the period of the crisis of 1837 occurred on the new frontier belt of the next tier of states. Thus each one of the periods of lax financial integrity coincides with periods when a new set of frontier communities had arisen, and coincides in area with these successive frontiers, for the most part. The recent Populist agitation is a case in point. Many a state that now declines any connection with the tenets of the Populists, itself adhered to such ideas in an earlier stage of the development of the state. A primitive society can hardly be expected to show the intelligent appreciation of the complexity of business interests in a developed society. The continual recurrence of these areas of paper-money agitation is another evidence that the frontier can be isolated and studied as a factor in American history of the highest importance.[46]

Attempts to Check and Regulate the Frontier

The East has always feared the result of an unregulated advance of the frontier, and has tried to check and guide it. The English authorities would have checked settlement at the headwaters of the Atlantic tributaries and allowed the "savages to enjoy their deserts in quiet lest the peltry trade should decrease." This called out Burke's splendid protest:

"If you stopped your grants, what would be the consequence: The people would occupy without grants. They have already so occupied in many places. You cannot station garrisons in every part of these deserts. If you drive the people from one place, they will carry on their annual tillage and remove with their flocks and herds to another. Many of the people in the back settlements are already little attached to particular situations. Already they have topped the Appalachian mountains. From thence they behold before them an immense plain, one vast, rich, level meadow; a square of five hundred miles. Over this they would wander without a possibility of restraint; they would change their manners with their habits of life; would soon forget a government by which they were disowned; would become hordes of English Tar-

tars; and, pouring down upon your unfortified frontiers a fierce and irresistible cavalry, become masters of your governors and your counselors, your collectors and comptrollers, and of all the slaves that adhered to them. Such would, and in no long time must, be the effect of attempting to forbid as a crime, and to suppress as an evil, the command and blessing of Providence, 'Increase and multiply.' Such would be the happy result of an endeavor to keep as a lair of wild beasts that earth which God, by an express charter, has given to the children of men."

But the English government was not alone in its desire to limit the advance of the frontier, and guide its destinies. Tidewater Virginia[47] and South Carolina[48] gerrymandered those colonies to ensure the dominance of the coast in their legislatures. Washington desired to settle a state at a time, in the Northwest; Jefferson would reserve from settlement the territory of his Louisiana purchase north of the 32^d parallel, in order to offer it to the Indians in exchange for their settlements east of the Mississippi. "When we shall be full on this side," he writes, "we may lay off a range of states on the western bank from the head to the mouth, and so range after range, advancing compactly as we multiply." Madison went so far as to argue to the French minister that the United States had no interest in seeing population extend itself on the right bank of the Mississippi, but should rather fear it. When the Oregon question was under debate, in 1824, Smyth, of Virginia, would draw an unchangeable line for the limits of the United States at the outer limit of two tiers of states beyond the Mississippi, complaining that the seaboard states were being drained of the flower of their population by the bringing of too much land into market. Even Thomas Benton, the man of widest views of the destiny of the West, at this stage of his career declared that along the ridge of the Rocky Mountains "the western limits of the republic should be drawn, and the statue of the fabled god Terminus should be raised upon its highest peak, never to be thrown down."[49] But the attempts to limit our boundaries, to restrict land sales and settlement, and to deprive the West of its share of political power, were all in vain. Steadily that frontier of settlement advanced and carried with it individualism, democracy and nationalism, and powerfully affected the Old World.

Missionary Activity

The most effective efforts of the East to regulate the frontier came through its educational and religious activity, exerted by interstate migration and by organized societies. Speaking in 1835, Dr. Lyman Beecher declared: "It is equally plain that the religious and political destiny of our nation is to be decided in the West," and he pointed out that the population of the West "is assembled from all the states of the Union, and from all the nations of Europe, and is rushing in like the waters of the flood, demanding for its moral preservation the immediate and universal action of those institutions which discipline the mind and arm the conscience and the heart. And so various are the opinions and habits, and so recent and imperfect is the acquaintance, and so sparse are the settlements of the West, that no homogeneous public sentiment can be formed to legislate immediately into being the requisite institutions. And yet they are all needed immediately in their utmost perfection and power. A nation is being 'born in a day.' . . . But what will become of the West if her prosperity rushes up to such a majesty of power, while those great institutions linger which are necessary to form the mind and the conscience, and the heart of that vast world. It must not be permitted . . . Let no man at the East quiet himself and dream of liberty, whatever may become of the West . . . Her destiny is our destiny."[50]

With this appeal to the conscience of New England, he adds appeals to her fears lest other religious sects anticipate her own. The New England preacher and school teacher left their mark on the West. The dread of western emancipation from New England's political and economic control was paralleled by fears lest the West cut loose from her religion. Commenting in 1850 on reports that settlement was rapidly extending northward in Wisconsin, the editor of *The Home Missionary* writes: "We scarcely know whether to rejoice or to mourn over this extension of our settlements. While we sympathize in whatever tends to increase the physical resources and prosperity of our country, we cannot forget that with all these dispersions into remote and still remoter corners of the land, the supply of the means of grace is becoming relatively less and less." Acting in accordance with such ideas, home missions were established and western colleges were erected. As seaboard cities like Philadelphia, New York, and Baltimore strove for the mastery of western trade, so the various denominations strove for the possession of the West. Thus an intellectual stream from New England sources fertilized the West. On the other hand, the contest for power and the expansive tendency, furnished to the various sects by the existence of a moving frontier, must have had important results on the character of religious organization in the United States. It is a chapter in our history which needs study.

Intellectual Traits

From the conditions of frontier life came intellectual traits of profound importance. The works of travellers along each frontier from colonial days onward describe for each certain traits, and these traits have, while softening down, still persisted as survivals in the place of their origin, even when a higher social organization succeeded. The result is that to the frontier the American intellect owes its striking characteristics. That coarseness and strength combined with acuteness and inquisitiveness, that practical, inventive turn of mind, quick to find expedients, that masterful grasp of material things, lacking in the artistic but powerful to effect great ends, that restless, nervous energy,[51] that dominant individualism, working for good and for evil, and withal that buoyancy and exuberance which comes with freedom—these are traits of the frontier, or traits called out elsewhere because of the existence of the frontier. Since the days when the fleet of Columbus sailed into the waters of the New World, America has been another name for opportunity, and the people of the United States have taken their tone from the incessant expansion which has not only been open but has even been forced upon them. He would be a rash prophet who should assert that the expansive character of American life has now entirely ceased. Movement has been its dominant fact, and, unless this training has no effect upon a people, the American intellect will continually demand a wider field for its exercise. But never again will such gifts of free land offer themselves. For a moment at the frontier the bonds of custom are broken, and unrestraint is triumphant. There is not *tabula rasa*. The stubborn American environment is there with its imperious summons to accept its conditions; the inherited ways of doing things are also there; and yet, in spite of environment, and in spite of custom, each frontier did indeed furnish a new field of opportunity, a gate of escape from the bondage of the past; and freshness, and confidence, and scorn of older society, impatience of its restraints and its ideas, and indifference to its lessons, have accompanied the frontier. What the Mediterranean Sea was to the Greeks, breaking the bond of custom, offering new experiences, calling out new institutions and activities, that, and more, the ever retreating frontier has been to the United States directly, and to the nations of Europe more remotely. And now, four centuries from the discovery of America, at the end of a hundred years of life under the Constitution, the frontier has gone, and with its going has closed the first period of American history.

Notes

1. The foundation of this paper is my article entitled, "Problems in American History," which appeared in *The Ægis,* a publication of the students of the University of Wisconsin, November 8, 1892. This address was first delivered at a meeting of the American Historical Association, in Chicago, July 12, 1893. It is gratifying to find that Professor Woodrow Wilson—whose volume on "Division and Reunion," in the *Epochs of American History* series, has an appreciative estimate of the importance of the West as a factor in American history—accepts some of the views set forth in the papers above mentioned, and enhances their value by his lucid and suggestive treatment of them in his article in *The Forum,* December, 1893, reviewing Goldwin Smith's *History of the United States.*

2. *Extra Census Bulletin,* No. 2, April 20, 1892.

3. *Abridgement of Debates of Congress,* v., p. 706.

4. *Bancroft* (1860 ed.), iii., pp. 344, 345, citing Logan MSS.; [Mitchell] *Contest in America,* etc. (1752), p. 237.

5. Kercheval, *History of the Valley;* Bernheim, *German Settlements in the Carolinas;* Winsor, *Narrative and Critical History of America,* v., p. 304; *Colonial Records of North Carolina,* iv., p. xx.; Weston, *Documents Connected with the History of South Carolina,* p. 82; Ellis and Evans, *History of Lancaster County, Pa.,* chs. iii., xxvi.

6. Parkman, *Pontiac,* ii.; Griffis, *Sir William Johnson,* p. 6; Simms's *Frontiersmen of New York.*

7. Monette, *Mississippi Valley,* i., p. 311.

8. *Wis. Hist. Colls.,* xi., p. 50; Hinsdale, *Old Northwest,* p., 121; Burke, "Oration on Conciliation," *Works* (1872 ed.), i., p. 473.

9. Roosevelt, *Winning of the West,* and citations there given; Cutler's *Life of Cutler.*

10. Scribner's *Statistical Atlas,* xxxviii., plate 13; MacMaster, *Hist. of People of U.S.,* i., pp. 4, 60, 61; Imlay and Filson, *Western Territory of America* (London, 1793); Rochefoucault-Liancourt, *Travels Through the United States of North America* (London, 1799); Michaux's "Journal," in *Proceedings of American Philosophical Society,* xxvii., No. 129; Forman, *Narrative of a Journey Down the Ohio and Mississippi in 1780–90* (Cincinnati, 1888); Bartram, *Travels Through North Carolina, etc.* (London, 1792); Pope, *Tour Through the Southern and Western Territories, etc.* (Richmond, 1792); Weld, *Travels Through the States of North America* (London, 1799); Baily, *Journal of a Tour in the Unsettled States of North America, 1796–7* (London, 1856); *Pennsylvania Magazine of History,* July, 1886; Winsor, *Narrative and Critical History of America,* vii., pp. 491, 492, citations.

11. Scribner's *Statistical Atlas,* xxxix.

12. Turner, *Character and Influence of the Indian Trade in Wisconsin* (Johns Hopkins University Studies, Series ix.), pp. 61 ff.

13. Monette, *History of the Mississippi Valley,* ii.; Flint, *Travels and Residence in Mississippi;* Flint, *Geography and History of the Western States; Abridgment of Debates of Congress,* vii., pp. 397, 398, 404; Holmes, *Account of the U.S.;* Kingdom, *America and the British Colonies* (London, 1820); Grund, *Americans,* ii., chs. i., iii., vi. (although writing

in 1836, he treats of conditions that grew out of western advance from the era of 1820 to that time); Peck, *Guide for Emigrants* (Boston, 1831); Darby, *Emigrants Guide to Western and Southwestern States and Territories;* Dana, *Geographical Sketches in the Western Country;* Kinzie, *Waubun;* Keating, *Narrative of Long's Expedition;* Schoolcraft, *Discovery of the Sources of the Mississippi River, Travels in the Central Portions of the Mississippi Valley,* and *Lead Mines of the Missouri;* Andreas, *History of Illinois,* i., 86–99; Hurlbut, *Chicago Antiquities;* McKenney, *Tour to the Lakes.*

14. Darby, *Emigrants' Guide,* pp. 272 ff.; Benton, *Abridgment of Debates,* vii., p. 397.

15. *DeBow's Review,* v., p. 254; xvii., p. 428.

16. Grund, *Americans,* ii., p. 8.

17. Peck, *New Guide to the West* (Cincinnati, 1848), ch. iv.; Parkman, *Oregon Trail;* Hall, *The West* (Cincinnati, 1848); Pierce, *Incidents of Western Travel;* Murray, *Travels in North America;* Lloyd, *Steamboat Directory* (Cincinnati, 1856); "Forty Days in a Western Hotel" (Chicago), in *Putnam's Magazine,* December, 1854; Mackay, *The Western World,* ii., ch. ii., iii.; Meeker, *Life in the West;* Bogen, *German in America* (Boston, 1851); Olmstead, *Texas Journey;* Greeley, *Recollections of a Busy Life;* Schouler, *History of United States,* v., 261–267; Peyton, *Over the Alleghanies and Across the Prairies* (London, 1870); Loughborough, *The Pacific Telegraph and Railway* (St. Louis, 1849); Whitney, *Project for a Railroad to the Pacific* (New York, 1849); Peyton, *Suggestions on Railroad Communication with the Pacific, and the Trade of China and the Indian Islands;* Benton, *Highway to the Pacific* (a speech delivered in the U.S. Senate, Dec. 16, 1850).

18. A writer in *The Home Missionary* (1850), p. 239, reporting Wisconsin conditions, exclaims: "Think of this, people of the enlightened East. What an example, to come from the very frontiers of civilization!" But one of the missionaries writes: "In a few years Wisconsin will no longer be considered as the West, or as an outpost of civilization, any more than Western New York, or the Western Reserve."

19. Bancroft (H.H.), *History of California, History of Oregon,* and *Popular Tribunals;* Shinn, *Mining Camps.*

20. See the suggestive paper by Prof. Jesse Macy, *The Institutional Beginnings of a Western State.*

21. Shinn, *Mining Camps.*

22. Compare Thorpe, in *Annals American Academy of Political and Social Science,* September, 1891; Bryce, *American Commonwealth* (1888), ii., p. 689.

23. Loria, *Analisi della Proprieta Capitalista,* ii., p. 15.

24. Compare *Observations on the North American Land Company,* London, 1796, pp. xv., 144; Logan, *History of Upper South Carolina,* i., pp. 149–151; Turner, *Character and Influence of Indian Trade in Wisconsin,* p. 18; Peck, *New Guide for Emigrants* (Boston, 1837), ch. iv.; *Compendium Eleventh Census,* i., p., xl.

25. But Lewis and Clark were the first to explore the route from the Missouri to the Columbia.

26. On the effect of the fur trade in opening the routes of migration, see the author's *Character and Influence of the Indian Trade in Wisconsin.*

27. Lodge, *English Colonies,* p. 152 and citations; Logan, *Hist. of Upper South Carolina,* i., p. 151.

28. Flint, *Recollections,* p. 9.

29. See Monette, *Mississippi Valley*, i., p. 344.

30. Coues's *Lewis and Clark's Expedition*, i., pp. 2, 253–259; Benton, in *Cong. Record*, xxiii., p. 57.

31. Hehn, *Das Salz* (Berlin, 1873).

32. *Col. Records of N. C.*, v., p. 3.

33. Finley, *Hist. of the Insurrection in the Four Western Counties of Pennsylvania in the Year 1794* (Philadelphia, 1796), p. 35.

34. Hale, *Daniel Boone*, etc., a pamphlet in the library of the State Historical Society of Wisconsin.

35. Compare Baily, *Tour in the Unsettled Parts of North America* (London, 1856), pp. 217–219, where a similar analysis is made for 1796.

36. "Spottswood Papers," in *Collections of Virginia Historical Society*, i., ii.

37. [Burke], *European Settlements*, etc. (1765 ed.), ii., p. 200.

38. *Wis. Hist. Colls.*, xii, pp. 7 ff.

39. Weston, *Documents connected with History of South Carolina*, p. 61.

40. See the admirable monograph by Prof. H. B. Adams, *Maryland's Influence on the Land Cessions*; and also Welling, in *Papers American Historical Association*, iii., p. 411.

41. Adams's *Memoirs*, ix., pp. 247, 248.

42. Author's article in *The Ægis*, Nov. 8, 1892.

43. *Political Science Quarterly*, ii., p. 457. Compare Sumner, *Alexander Hamilton*, chs. ii.–vii.

44. Compare Wilson, *Division and Reunion*, pp. 15, 24.

45. On the relation of frontier conditions to Revolutionary taxation, see Sumner, *Alexander Hamilton*, ch. iii.

46. I have refrained from dwelling on the lawless characteristics of the frontier, because they are sufficiently well known. The gambler and desperado, the regulators of the Carolinas and the vigilantes of California, are types of that line of scum that the waves of advancing civilization bore before them, and of the growth of spontaneous organs of authority where legal authority was absent. Compare Barrows, *United States of Yesterday and To-morrow*; Shinn, *Mining Camps*; and Bancroft, *Popular Tribunals*. The humor, bravery, and rude strength, as well as the vices of the frontier in its worst aspect, have left traces on American character, language, and literature, not soon to be effaced.

47. *Debates in the Constitutional Convention*, 1829–1830.

48. [McCrady] *Eminent and Representative Men of the Carolinas*, i., p. 43.

49. *Speech in the Senate*, March 1, 1825; *Register of Debates*, i., 721.

50. *Plea for the West* (Cincinnati, 1835), pp. 11 ff.

51. Colonial travellers agree in remarking on the phlegmatic characteristics of the colonists. It has frequently been asked how such a people could have developed that strained nervous energy now characteristic of them. Compare Sumner, *Alexander Hamilton*, p. 98, and Adams's *History of the United States*, i., p. 60; ix., pp. 240, 241. The transition appears to become marked at the close of the War of 1812, a period when interest centered upon the development of the West, and the West was noted for restless energy. Grund, *Americans*, ii., ch. 1.

The Significance of the Section
in American History

A GENERATION AGO I PUBLISHED in the *Proceedings* of this Society a paper which I had read at the summer meeting of the American Historical Association, on "The Significance of the Frontier in American History." The Superintendent of the Census had just announced that a frontier line could no longer be traced, and had declared: "In the discussion of its extent, its westward movement, etc., it cannot therefore any longer have a place in the census reports."

The significance in American history of the advance of the frontier and of its disappearance is now generally recognized. This evening I wish to consider with you another fundamental factor in American history, namely, the Section. Arising from the facts of physical geography and the regional settlement of different peoples and types of society on the Atlantic coast there was a sectionalism from the beginning. But soon this became involved and modified by the fact that these societies were expanding into the interior, following the frontier, and that their sectionalism took special forms in the presence of the growing West. Today we are substantially a settled nation without the overwhelming influence that accompanied the westward spread of population. Urban concentration chiefly in the East has reversed the movement to a considerable extent. We are more like Europe, and our sections are becoming more and more the American version of the European nation.

First let us consider the influence of the frontier and the West upon American sections. Until our own day, as I urged in that paper, the United States was always beginning over on its outer edge as it advanced into the wilderness. Therefore the United States was both a developed and a primitive society. The West was a migrating region, a stage of society rather than a place. Each region reached in the process of expansion from the coast had its frontier experience, was for a time "the West," and when the frontier passed on to new regions, it left behind in the older areas, memories, traditions, an inherited attitude toward life, that persisted long after the frontier had passed by. But while the influence of the frontier permeated East as well as West, by survival of the pioneer psychology and by the reaction of the Western ideals and life upon the East, it was in the newer regions, in the area called the West at any given time, that frontier traits and conceptions were most in evidence. This "West" was more than "the frontier" of popular speech. It included also the more populous transitional zone adjacent, which was still influenced by pioneer traditions and where economic society had more in common with the newer than with the older regions.

This "West" wherever found at different years thought of itself and of the nation in different ways from those of the East. It needed capital; it was a debtor region, while the East had the capital and was a creditor section. The West was rural, agricultural, while the East was becoming more and more urban and industrial. Living under conditions where the family was the self-sufficing economic unit, where the complications of more densely settled society did not exist, without accumulated inherited wealth, the frontier regions stressed the rights of man, while the statesmen who voiced the interests of the East stressed the rights of property.

The West believed in the rule of the majority, in what John Randolph, the representative of the Virginia tidewater aristocracy, called "King Numbers." The East feared an unchecked democracy, which might overturn minority rights, destroy established institutions, and attack vested interests. The buoyant, opti-

mistic, and sometimes reckless and extravagant spirit of innovation was the very life of the West. In the East innovation was a
term of reproach. It always "stalked" like an evil spirit. The East
represented accumulated experience, the traditions of the family
living generation after generation in a single location and under a
similar environment, as President Thwing, of Western Reserve
University, has aptly put it. But out in the newer West through
most of its history men lived in at least two or three states in the
course of their migrations. Of the hundred and twenty-four
members of the first Wisconsin constitutional convention in 1846,
the average was three states for each member. Four had moved
eight times. Sixteen had lived in five or more different states, or
foreign countries and states; six had lived in seven or more.

The West demanded cheap or free lands on which to base a
democratic farming population. The ruling interests in the East
feared that such a policy would decrease land values at home and
diminish the value of lands which its capitalists had purchased for
speculation in the interior. It feared that cheap lands in the West
would draw Eastern farmers into the wilderness; would break
down the bonds of regular society; would prevent effective control of the discontented; would drain the labor supply away from
the growing industrial towns, and thus raise wages.

The West opened a refuge from the rule of established classes,
from the subordination of youth to age, from the sway of established and revered institutions. Writing in 1694 when the frontier
lay at the borders of Boston Bay, the Reverend Cotton Mather
asked: "Do our *Old* People any of them *Go Out* from the Institutions of God, swarming into New Settlements where they and
their Untaught Families are like *to Perish for Lack of Vision?*" To
their cost, he said, such men have "got unto the *Wrong side of the
Hedge*" and "the Angel of the Lord becomes their enemy."

No doubt all this makes too sharply contrasted a picture. But
from the beginning East and West have shown a sectional attitude. The interior of the colonies on the Atlantic was disrespectful
of the coast, and the coast looked down upon the upland folk. The

"Men of the Western World" when they crossed the Alleghanies became self-conscious and even rebellious against the rule of the East. In the thirties the tidewater aristocracy was conquered by the Jacksonian Democracy of the interior.

And so one could go on through the story of the anti-monopolists, the Grangers, the Populists, the Insurgents, the Progressives, the Farmers' Bloc, and the La Follette movement, to illustrate the persistence of the sectionalism of the West, or of considerable parts of it, against the East.

Perhaps Eastern apprehension was never more clearly stated than by Gouverneur Morris of Pennsylvania in the Constitutional Convention of 1787. "The busy haunts of men, not the remote wilderness," said he, are "the proper school of political talents. If the western people get the power into their hands they will ruin the Atlantic interests. The back members are always averse to the best measures." He would so fix the ratio of representation that the number of representatives from the Atlantic States should always be larger than the number from the Western States. This, he argued, would not be unjust "as the Western settlers would previously know the conditions on which they were to possess their lands." So influential was his argument that the convention struck out the provision in the draft which guaranteed equality with the old states to the states thereafter to be admitted to the Union. But on the motion that the representatives from new states should not exceed those from the Old Thirteen, the affirmative vote was cast by Massachusetts, Connecticut, Delaware, and Maryland; Pennsylvania was divided; and the motion was defeated by the votes of the Southern States plus New Jersey.

To the average American, to most American historians, and to most of the writers of our school textbooks (if one can trust the indexes to their books) the word *section* applies only to the struggle of South against North on the questions of slavery, state sovereignty, and, eventually, disunion.

But the Civil War was only the most drastic and most tragic of sectional manifestations, and in no small degree the form which it took depended upon the fact that rival societies, free and slave, were marching side by side into the unoccupied lands of the West, each attempting to dominate the back country, the hinterland, working out agreements from time to time, something like the diplomatic treaties of European nations, defining spheres of influence, and awarding mandates, such as in the Missouri Compromise, the Compromise of 1850, and the Kansas-Nebraska Act. Each Atlantic section was, in truth, engaged in a struggle for power; and power was to be gained by drawing upon the growing West. In the Virginia ratification convention of 1787 William Grayson, by no means the most radical of the members, said: "I look upon this as a contest for empire. . . . If the Mississippi be shut up, emigrations will be stopped entirely. There will be no new states formed on the Western Waters. . . .This contest of the Mississippi involves the great national contest; that is whether one part of this continent shall govern the other. The Northern States have the majority and will endeavor to retain it." Similar conceptions abound in the utterances of North Atlantic statesmen. "It has been said," declared Morris in 1787, "that North Carolina, South Carolina and Georgia only, will in a little time have a majority of the people of America. They must in that case include the great interior country and everything is to be apprehended from their getting power into their hands."

If time permitted, it would be possible to illustrate by such utterances all through our history to very recent times how the Eastern sections regarded the West with its advancing frontier as the raw material for power. To New England until her own children began to occupy the prairies ("reserved by God," as her pioneers declared, "for a pious and industrious people") this aspect of the West threatened to enable the South perpetually to rule the nation. The first great migration, the most extensive in the area covered, flowed into the interior from the Southern upland. Some of the extreme leaders of the New England Federalists did not so much desire to break away from the South as to deprive that section of the three-fifths representation for its slaves, and either to permit the Western States to leave the Union or to see them won by England. Then the Old Thirteen could be united under conditions which would check the expansion of the South and would leave New England in control.

Writing in 1786 Rufus King, of New York, later senator and minister to England, while admitting that it was impolitic at the time wholly to give up the Western settlers, declared that very few men who had examined the subject would refuse their assent "to the opinion that every Citizen of the Atlantic States, who emigrates to the westward of the Alleghany is a total loss to our confederacy."

"Nature," he said, "has severed the two countries by a vast and extensive chain of mountains, interest and convenience will keep them separate, and the feeble policy of our disjointed Government will not be able to unite them. For these reasons I have ever been opposed to encouragements of western emigrants. The States situated on the Atlantic are not sufficiently populous, and losing our men is losing our greatest source of wealth."

Of course the immediate complaint in New England and New York was against the South itself, its Jeffersonian principles, so antagonistic to New England Puritanism; its slavery, its pro-French sympathies. But all these gained much of their force by the conviction that the West was a reservoir from which the South would continue to draw its power. Among the proposals of the Hartford Convention was that no new state should be admitted into the Union without the concurrence of two-thirds of both houses of Congress. The report warned the old states against "an overwhelming Western influence" and predicted that "finally the Western States, multiplied in numbers and augmented in population will control the interests of the whole." Had this proposed amendment been made, the New England States with two other states in the Senate could have blocked the West from future statehood. Nathan Dane, after whom Dane County in this state is named, furnished the argument for this proposal by his elaborate tabulations and schedules. He pointed out that in the commercial states capital was invested in commerce, and in the slave-holding states in western lands. When "Kentucky, Ohio, and Tennessee were raised up by this interest & admitted into the Union, then the balance was, materially, affected. The non-commercial states pressed the admission of Louisiana and turned the balance against the Northeast." "It clearly follows," he reasoned, "that if a bare majority in Congress can admit new States into the union (all interior ones as they must be) at pleasure, in these immense Western regions, the balance of the union as once fairly contemplated, must soon be destroyed."

But Jackson defeated the British at New Orleans. The Mississippi Valley remained within the Union, Louisiana's interests became affiliated with the commercial states in many ways, and New England people poured so rapidly into the West that New England found in the northern half of the Valley the basis for a new alliance and new power as disturbing to the slaveholding South as the Southern and Western connection had been to New England.

By the middle of the century the South was alarmed at the Western power much in the way that New England had been. "I have very great fears," wrote Justice Campbell, later of the Federal Supreme Court, from Mobile to Calhoun in 1847, "that the existing territories of the United States will prove too much for our government. The wild and turbulent conduct of the members upon the Oregon question and their rapacity and greediness in all matters connected with the appropriation of the revenues induces great doubt of the propriety of introducing new States in the Union so fast as we do." Of the legislators from the Western States he said, "Their notions are freer, their impulses stronger, their wills less restrained. I do not wish to increase the number till the New States already admitted to the Union become civilized."

On the other hand, it must be clearly borne in mind that as the West grew in power of population and in numbers of new senators, it resented the conception that it was merely an emanation from a rival North and South; that it was the dependency of one or another of the Eastern sections; that it was to be so limited and controlled as to maintain an equilibrium in the Senate between North and South. It took the attitude of a section itself.

From the beginning the men who went west looked to the future when the people beyond the Alleghanies should rule the nation. Dr. Manasseh Cutler, the active promoter of the Ohio Company of Associates, which made the first considerable permanent settlement in the Old Northwest Territory, wrote in 1787 a *Description of Ohio.* Though himself the minister at Ipswich in the heart of that stronghold of conservatism, the "Essex Junto," he declared that on the Ohio would be "the seat of empire" for the whole Union. Within twenty years, he predicted, there would be more people on the western side of the Alleghany watershed than in the East, and he congratulated these people that "in order to begin right there will be no wrong habits to combat and no inveterate systems to overturn—there will be no rubbish to remove before you lay the foundations." Evidently it did not take long to produce the Western point of view.

In the Senate in 1837 Benton, of Missouri, scorned the proposals of Calhoun regarding the disposition of the public domain, and boasted that after the census of 1840 had shown the weight of the West it would be so highly bid for that it would write its own bill. Perhaps the debate over the Compromise of 1850 brings out the self-assertive Western attitude in these years most clearly. Calhoun had argued that the equilibrium between North and South was being destroyed by the increase in free states made out of the Western territories. But Stephen A. Douglas, of Illinois, spoke for the West when he attacked the Southern statesman for the error of thinking of the West as property of the older sections. "What share had the South in the territories," he asked, "or the North, or any other geographical division unknown to the Constitution? I answer none—none at all." And Douglas calculated that if its right to self-determination were admitted, the West

would form at least seventeen new free states, and that therefore
the theory of equilibrium was a hopeless one.

It was not only the slavery struggle that revealed the Eastern
conception of the West as merely the field of contest for power
between the rival Atlantic sections, and the West's counter asser-
tion of its own substantive rights. The same thing was shown in
many different fields. For example rival Eastern cities and states,
the centers of power in their respective sections, engaged in contests for the commercial control of the Mississippi Valley by transportation lines. The contests between rival European powers for
the control of the Bagdad railway, the thrust of Germany toward
the rich hinterlands made up of the Balkans and India, and the
project of *Central Europe* in the history of the World War, have a
resemblance to these American sectional contests for the still
more valuable hinterland of the Mississippi Valley. American sections did not go to war over their trade and transportation interests. Nevertheless they recognized that there were such interests.
A Southern writer in *DeBow's Review* in 1847 declared:

"A contest has been going on between the North and South not
limited to slavery or no slavery—to abolition or no abolition, nor
to the politics of either whigs or democrats as such, but a contest
for the wealth and commerce of the great valley of the Mississippi—a contest tendered by our Northern brethren, whether the
growing commerce of the great West shall be thrown upon New
Orleans or given to the Atlantic cities."

Shortly after this, in 1851, the *Western Journal* of St. Louis published articles lamenting that "the Western States are subjected to
the relation of Provinces of the East" and that New Orleans was
giving way to New York as their commercial city. Since (so the
argument ran) exports can never build up a commercial city, the
mouth of the Mississippi must be so improved that imports would
enter the Valley by way of New Orleans. "Then," said the writer,
"a line of cities will arise on the banks of the Mississippi that will
far eclipse those on the Atlantic coast.

The middle of the century saw an extension of this sectional contest for economic power derived from the growing West; but it was the railroad trunk lines rather than the canals that occupied the foreground. The goal became the ports of the Pacific. The Memphis convention of 1845 and the Chicago convention of 1847 illustrate how interior cities were now repeating the rivalry for western trade which had earlier been seen on the Atlantic coast. The contests between New Orleans, Memphis, St. Louis, and Chicago influenced the Kansas-Nebraska Act, and the later strategy of the struggle for position between the Pacific railroads.

Throughout our history, then, there has been this sectionalism of West and East, and this Eastern conception of the West as recruiting ground merely for the rival Atlantic coast sections. Nation-wide parties have had their eastern and western wings, often differing radically, and yet able by party loyalty and by adjustments and sacrifices to hold together. Such a struggle as the slavery contest can only be understood by bearing in mind that it was not merely a contest of North against South, but that its form and its causes were fundamentally shaped by the dynamic factor of expanding sections, of a West to be won.

This migratory sectionalism has not always been obvious, but it was none the less real and important. Year after year new Wests had been formed. Wildernesses equal in area to the greater European nations had been turned into farms in single decades.

But now the era of the frontier advance has ended. The vast public domain, so far as it is suited to agriculture, is taken up. The competent experts of the Department of Agriculture now tell us that "the nation reached and passed the apogee of agricultural land supply in proportion to population in 1890, and that we have entered a period which will necessarily be marked by a continually increasing scarcity of land." The price of lands has risen as the supply of free lands declined. Iowa farm lands mounted from an average of thirty dollars per acre in 1890 to over two hundred dollars in 1920.

Shortly after 1890 men began to speak less confidently of the inexhaustible forest supply. The reclamation act early in the twentieth century began a new era in governmental conservation and governmental economic activity. The Conservation Congress met in 1908, three centuries after the Jamestown settlers sank their axes into the edge of the American forest. The purpose of the congress was to consider the menace of forest exhaustion, the waste of soil fertility and of mineral resources, the reclamation of the deserts, the drainage of the swamps. Now we are told by high authority that we shall feel the pinch of timber shortage in less than fifteen years. The free lands are no longer free; the boundless resources are no longer boundless. Already the urban population exceeds the rural population of the United States.

But this does not mean that the Eastern industrial type of urban life will necessarily spread across the whole nation, for food must come from somewhere, and the same expert authorities that predict that within about fifty years the United States itself will be unable to feed its population by its home supply, also conclude that the deficient food supply will not be available from outside the nation, because the same phenomenon of the encroachment of population upon food is in evidence throughout the world. Already Europe as a whole depends upon importation for its food supply. Its large population in proportion to its area and resources cannot be made the basis for estimates of what is possible in the United States, for Europe's large population was made possible by these imports from the United States as well as from other nations.

If the prediction be true, or if anything like it be true, then there must remain in the United States large rural farming interests and sections. The natural advantages of certain regions for farming, or for forestry, or for pasturage will arrest the tendency of the Eastern industrial type of society to flow across the continent and thus to produce a consolidated, homogeneous nation free from sections. At the same time that the nation settles down to the conditions of an occupied land, there will be emphasized the sectional differences arising from unlike geographic regions.

To President Coolidge, as a speech of his in November last

shows, the prospect is of a nation importing its supplies of food and resources, facing "the problem of maintaining a prosperous, self-reliant, confident agriculture in a country preponderantly commercial and industrial." Whether our destiny is to become a nation in which agriculture is subordinate, or one in which it is an equal partner with urban industrial interests, it seems clear that there will be sectional expression of the differences between these interests; for in certain geographic provinces agriculture will be entirely subordinate to manufacture, as in others such industry will be insignificant as compared with farming.

Unlike such countries as France and Germany, the United States has the problem of the clash of economic interests closely associated with regional geography on a huge scale. Over areas equal to all France or to all Germany, either the agricultural or the manufacturing types are here in decided ascendancy. Economic interests are sectionalized. The sections occupied by a rural population are of course far inferior in numbers of voters to the sections of urban industrial life. The map is deceptive in this respect, for Greater New York City, which would be a point on the map, has almost as many people as live in all the vast spaces of the Mountain and Pacific States. The population of the New England States and the Middle States of the North Atlantic division is over thirty millions, while the population of Wisconsin, Minnesota, North and South Dakota, Montana, Wyoming, Idaho, Washington, and Oregon is less than ten millions. On the map these states take an imposing space, but owing to physical geography a large portion will always remain sparsely settled. Nevertheless New England and the Middle States together have only eighteen senators, while the states of the section which I have just named have also eighteen senators. New York State alone has a larger population than this northwestern zone of states; but this wealthy and populous state has only two senators as against the eighteen senators of the other region.

On a map constructed so as to give to each state a space proportioned to its population, or to its income tax, instead of to its dimensions in square miles, the western lands would shrink in their map space in a startling fashion. But in the Senate is exhibited the outcome of the tendencies which statesmen like Gouverneur Morris saw so clearly, namely, the great power of the newer states by their equal representation in the Senate and their ability to take property by taxation from the wealthier section and to distribute it according to numbers, or even according to deficiencies, throughout the Union as a unit. Obviously there is here the certainty of a sectional clash of interests, not unlike those which led to Calhoun's South Carolina Exposition.

Sectionalism will hereafter be shaped by such new forces. We have become a nation comparable to all Europe in area, with settled geographic provinces which equal great European nations. We are in this sense an empire, a federation of sections, a union of potential nations. It is well to look at the result of our leap to power since the ending of the frontier in order to appreciate our problems arising from size and varied sections.

We raise three-fourths of the world's corn, over a third of its swine, over half its cotton, and over one-fifth its wheat. Out of the virgin wilderness we have built such industrial power that we now produce two-thirds of the pig-iron of the world, over twice the steel tonnage of England, Germany, and France combined. We mine nearly half the world's coal. We have fully half the gold coin and bullion of the world, and in 1920 our national wealth exceeded the combined wealth of the United Kingdom, France, and Germany. In the World War President Wilson gave the word that sent two million Americans across the seas to turn the scale in that Titanic conflict. We are forced to think of ourselves continentally and to compare ourselves with all Europe. Why, with so vast a territory, with so many geographic provinces, equal in area, in natural resources, and in natural variety to the lands of the great nations of Europe, did we not become another Europe? What tendencies have we developed that resembled those of Europe in

the course of our history? Are there tendencies toward the transformation of our great sections into types similar to European
nations?

It was evident at the outset of a study of the frontier movement
that the American people were not passing into a monotonously
uniform space. Rather, even in the colonial period, they were en-
tering successive different geographic provinces; they were pouring their plastic pioneer life into geographic moulds. They would
modify these moulds, they would have progressive revelations of
the capacities of the geographic provinces which they won and
settled and developed; but even the task of dealing constructively
with the different regions would work its effects upon their traits.

Not a uniform surface, but a kind of checkerboard of differing
environments, lay before them in their settlement. There would
be the interplay of the migrating stocks and the new geographic
provinces. The outcome would be a combination of the two factors, land and people, the creation of differing societies in the different sections. European nations were discovered, conquered,
colonized, and developed so far back in history that the process of
nation-making is obscure. Not so with section-making in the
United States. The process has gone on almost under our own
observation. But by the bondage to the modern map, as John
Fiske put it, much American history has been obscured. Our constitutional forms, in contrast with realities, provide for a federation of states. Our historians have dealt chiefly with local history,
state history, national history, and but little with sectional history.
Our students of government have been more aware of the legal
relations of states and nation than with the actual groupings of
states into sections, and with the actions of these sections beneath
the political surface. State sovereignty, for example, has in fact
never been a vital issue except when a whole section stood behind
the challenging state. This is what gave the protest reality.

One of the most interesting features of recent geographical
studies is the emphasis placed upon regional geography and hu-

man geography. Europe has given more attention to such studies in human geography than has the United States. Perhaps this is because European nations have been forced to consider the geographical aspects of the self-determination of nations and the rearrangement of the map by the treaty which seemed to close the World War. Perhaps in the hard realities of that war the military staffs and the scientists who had to deal with the problem of supplies of food and of raw material were compelled to give attention to the subject. But even before and after this war, the increasing pressure of population upon the means of life compelled in Europe the study of the natural regions, their resources and peoples, and their relations to each other. Now the conditions which I have been attempting to make clear in the United States are forcing us to face the same problem. We, like European nations, are approaching a saturation of population.

That sectionalism which is based on geographical regions has been in evidence from the early colonial period, but it has been obscured and modified by the influence of the unoccupied West. The states have been declining and are likely to continue to diminish in importance in our politics; but the groups of states called sections are likely to become more significant as the state declines. A study of votes in the federal House and Senate from the beginning of our national history reveals the fact that party voting has more often broken down than maintained itself on fundamental issues; that when these votes are mapped or tabulated by the congressional districts or states from which those who cast them came, instead of by alphabetical arrangement, a persistent sectional pattern emerges.

There has been in the earlier periods the sharp clash between New England and the South, with the Middle States divided and unstable, constituting a buffer zone and often holding the balance of power. Then as population spread westward the greater parties were composed of sectional wings—normally in the Republican party there came to be a fairly solid conservative New England, a mixed and uncertain Middle Region, and a more radical North Central wing, ready in the shaping of legislation to join the Democrats in a kind of sectional bloc (even before the days of the bloc) to oppose the conservative and dominant Eastern wing. As time went on, the East North Central States came into closer connection with the Eastern wing, and in the West North Central lay the areas of radical dissent and of third-party movements. Legislation was determined less by party than by sectional voting. Bills were shaped for final passage by compromises between wings or by alliances between sections. The maps of presidential elections showing majorities by counties look like maps of North against South; but there was always a concealed East and West which temporarily laid aside their differences.

I think it not too much to say that in party conventions as well as Congress the outcome of deliberations bears a striking resemblance to treaties between sections, suggestive of treaties between European nations in diplomatic congresses. But over an area equal to all Europe we found it possible to legislate, and we tempered asperities and avoided wars by a process of sectional give-and-take. Whether we shall continue to preserve our national, our inter-sectional, party organization in the sharper sectional conflicts of interest that are likely to accompany the settling down of population, the completer revelation of the influence of physical geography, remains to be seen.

As an illustration of the newer forms of sectionalism, take the movement for the Great Lakes-St. Lawrence deep waterway. Middle Western leaders are arguing that there is "in the heart of the continent a large area beyond the radius of logical rail haul for the movement of bulk commodities to either seacoast." "Nature," runs the argument, "which has indicated the extent of the area which sends its surplus to the Atlantic seaboard and to the Gulf and to the Pacific ports, has provided the American continent with one potential seacoast not yet utilized. Upon the map of economic divides indicated by geography—the Atlantic seaboard, the Gulf territory, and the Pacific slope—there is, as it were, an economic desert a thousand miles east and west, five hundred miles north and south beyond the radius of logical rail haul to either coast." The desire to give an outlet to what is called this "landlocked commerce to the coast," leads to the demand for "a fourth economic divide based upon the Great Lakes as linked with the ocean, giving to the coast of the Great Lakes access to marine commerce" and permitting the erection of each rail system upon the sea base.[1]

When ex-Senator Townsend of Michigan was running for re-election a Detroit daily reported: "The East is opposed to him because of his leadership in the waterways movement, but the entire West from Ohio to Idaho is looking hopefully and earnestly to Michigan to give him the largest majority he has ever received. The east and the west will be 'listening in' election night—the east hoping for a reduced Townsend vote, the west hoping fervently that his vote will be a knockout blow to the eastern opposition to the St. Lawrence waterway."

I quote this to take the opportunity to point out that sweeping statements like these exaggerate the sectional feeling. As a matter of fact, of course, very few Eastern voters knew much about Townsend, and, east and west, most of the radio fans were listening in to the vaudeville or the football game or the real prize fight.

But while Duluth writers press the importance of what they call this "frustrated seaway," New York writers protest that the outlet should be through an enlarged Erie Canal if there is to be such a water route at all, and it is argued that the projected St. Lawrence route would be "Our Dardanelles," liable to be closed against the West by Canadian or British government whenever disagreements invited this mode of coercion. In New England meantime there are fears that Boston would be injured as a port, besides the loss of her advantages by sea-borne commerce to the Pacific coast. A few years ago Mayor Curley of Boston indignantly declared that such a waterway "would obliterate New England absolutely."

I read the other day editorials in the *Chicago Tribune* which made the decision of the Supreme Court against the claim of the sanitary district to divert water from Lake Michigan without the permission of the Secretary of War the occasion for this language: "It is time for Chicago, Illinois, and the entire Mississippi Valley to rise in revolt against a tyranny which now threatens its very existence . . . . This is neither a conquered country nor a colony but an integral part of a nation, and as such entitled to the same consideration afforded to New England and New York." The editorial goes on to demand action to prevent the houses of Congress from organizing, etc. In another editorial of that issue, under the caption "The West is West, but the East is London," it is said: "It is natural that the East should turn to London for London policy is Atlantic policy," and the editor speaks of "London and its provinces in Montreal, Boston, New York and Washington."

No doubt this language is not to be taken with entire seriousness, but it is vigorous enough. It proposes revolt, and paralysis of government; and it, in effect, reads a rather substantial chunk of America out of the Union. Allowing for New England's restraint in speech, mildly similar utterances can be found in the press of that section whenever its interests seem threatened by West or South.[2] When Senator John Taylor, of Virginia, informed Jefferson that the Northeast felt that union with the South was doomed to fail, that philosophic statesman replied in words that are worthy of extended quotation as illustrating both a tolerant spirit and an amusing impression of New England:

"It is true that we are completely under the saddle of Massachusetts and Connecticut and that they ride us very hard, cruelly insulting our feelings, as well as exhausting our strength and substance. Their natural friends, the three other eastern states, join them from a sort of family pride, and they have the art to divide certain other parts of the Union so as to make use of them to govern the whole." But "seeing," said Jefferson, "that an association of men who will not quarrel with one another is a thing which never existed... seeing we must have somebody to quarrel with, I had rather keep our New England associates for that purpose than to see our bickerings transferred to others. They are circumscribed within such narrow bounds, and their population is so full, that their numbers will ever be in the minority, and they are marked, like the Jews, with such perversity of character, as to constitute from that circumstance the natural division of our parties." It will be observed that although he does not extol New England he does not read her out of the Union. The significant fact is that sectional self-consciousness and sensitiveness is likely to be increased as time goes on and crystallized sections feel the full influence of their geographic peculiarities, their special interests, and their developed ideals, in a closed and static nation.

There is a sense in which sectionalism is inevitable and desirable. There is and always has been a sectional geography in America based fundamentally upon geographic regions. There is a geography of political habit—a geography of opinion, of material interests, of racial stocks, of physical fitness, of social traits, of literature, of the distribution of men of ability, even of religious denominations. Professor Josiah Royce defined a "province" or section, in the sense in which I am using the word, as "any one part of a national domain which is geographically and socially sufficiently unified to have a true consciousness of its own ideals and customs and to possess a sense of its distinction from other parts of the country." It was the opinion of this eminent philosopher that the world needs now more than ever before the vigorous development of a highly organized provincial life to serve as a check upon mob psychology on a national scale, and to furnish that variety which is essential to vital growth and originality. With this I agree. But I wish also to urge here, as I have elsewhere, that there is always the danger that the province or section shall think of itself naively as the nation, that New England shall think that

America is merely New England writ large, or the Middle West shall think that America is really the Middle West writ large, and then proceed to denounce the sections that do not perceive the accuracy of this view as wicked or ignorant and un-American. This kind of nationalism is a sectional mirage, but it is common, and has been common to all the sections in their unconscious attitude if not in clear expression. It involves the assumption of a superiority of culture, of *Kultur,* to which good morals require that the nation as a whole must yield.

We must frankly face the fact that in this vast and heterogeneous nation, this sister of all Europe, regional geography is a fundamental fact; that the American peace has been achieved by restraining sectional selfishness and assertiveness and by coming to agreements rather than to reciprocal denunciation or to blows.

In the past we have held our sections together partly because while the undeveloped West was open there was a safety valve, a region for hopeful restoration; partly because there were national political parties, calling out national party allegiance and loyalty over all sections and at the same time yielding somewhat under stress to sectional demands. Party was like an elastic band.

But there would often have been serious danger, such as showed itself when parties became definitely sectionalized just before the Civil War, had it not been the fact that popular party majorities over most of the sections are much closer than is usually supposed. The party held its tenure of power by a narrow margin and must use its power temperately or risk defeat. It must conciliate sectional differences within itself.

Not only the narrowness of normal party majorities, county by county over the nation, but also the existence within each of the large sections of smaller sections or regions which did not agree with the views of their section as a whole, constituted a check both upon party despotism and upon sectional arrogance and exploitation of other sections.

In every state of the Union there are geographic regions,

chiefly, but not exclusively, those determined by the ancient forces of geology, which divide the state into the lesser sections. These subsections within the states often cross state lines and connect with like areas in neighboring states and even in different sections of the larger type. Many states have now been made the subject of monographic studies of their internal sections shown in party politics, in economic interests, in social types, in cultural matters such as education, literature, and religion. I have prepared such maps of the United States for the year 1850. For example, the map by counties showing the distribution of white illiteracy so closely resembles the map of the physiographic regions that the one might almost be taken for the other. Much the same is true for the map of farm values by counties. I have also mapped the Whig and Democratic counties in the presidential elections from 1836 to 1852 and combined them in a map, which shows that certain regions, certain groups of counties, were almost always Whig and others normally Democratic through all these years. Then I have had the photographer superimpose these maps one upon another. As a result it is shown that the rough, the poorer lands, the illiterate counties were for the most part the Democratic counties; while the fertile basins—like the richer wheat areas of the Old Northwest, the limestone islands about Lexington, Kentucky, and Nashville, Tennessee, the Black Belt of the Gulf States, the center of the cotton and slavery interests, the abode of the wealthy and educated great slaveholding planters—were Whig. The Whigs tended to be strong in the areas of the greater rivers and commercial centers and routes, and in the counties with the better record in the matter of illiteracy.

Now I am not saying that Democracy and illiteracy and poor soils are necessarily connected. One of the interesting results of the study is to show that there were exceptions that prevent any such exclusively physical explanations. In North Carolina, for example, very notable Whig areas were in the most illiterate, rough, mountainous counties of that state, where the poor whites were antagonistic to the wealthy slaveholding Democratic planters of the eastern counties. Certain regions, like western New York and the Western Reserve of Ohio, show not so much the influence of physical geography as of the fact that they were colonized by New Englanders and carried on the interest in vested rights which distinguished the Puritan stock.

In short, the studies show that generalizations which make physical geography or economic interests alone the compelling explanation of political groupings are mistaken. There are also the factors of ideals and psychology, the inherited intellectual habits, derived from the stock from which the voters sprang. Sometimes these ideals carry the voters into lines that contradict their economic interests. But as a rule there has been such a connection of the stock, the geographic conditions, the economic interests, and the conceptions of right and wrong, that all have played upon each other to the same end.

Next I wish to emphasize the fact that these regional subdivisions are persistent. Often they remain politically the same for several generations. Probably the mass of voters inherit their party and their political ideas. Habit rather than reasoning is the fundamental factor in determining political affiliation of the mass of voters, and there is a geography, a habitat, of political habit.

There is the same geography of culture, though I am not able in the time that remains to develop this. For example, in a recent map of short-story areas (of what the author calls local color areas) almost exactly the same regions are shown as appear on the maps which I have mentioned.

There is, then, a sectionalism of the regions within the larger divisions, a sectionalism of minority areas, sometimes protesting against the policies of the larger section in which they lie and finding more in common with similar regions outside of this section. Herein lies a limitation upon the larger section in case it attempts a drastic and subversive policy toward other sections. As Professor Holcombe has pointed out, in this kind of nation, in this vast congeries of sections, voters cannot hope to have a choice between parties any one of which will stand for all the measures which they oppose. The most they can reasonably hope for, he thinks, "is the formation of a party, resting upon a combination of sectional interests which are capable of cooperation in national politics without too much jealousy and friction, and including that particular interest with which they are themselves most closely associated. No sectional interest is strong enough, alone and unaided, to control the federal government, and no major party can be formed with a fair prospect of domination in national politics which does not contain more or less incongruous elements."

With this I agree, and indeed have long been on record to this effect. It emphasizes the need for tolerance, for cooperation, for mutual sacrifices by the leaders of the various sections. Statesmanship in this nation consists not only in representing the special interests of the leader's own section, but in finding a formula that will bring the different regions together in a common policy. The greatest statesmen have always had this goal before them. If there were time I should like to quote the striking confirmation of this in writings of even such men as John Quincy Adams, Van Buren, and Calhoun, who are ordinarily thought of as rather definitely sectional. Each formulated plans for concessions to the various sections whereby a national pattern could emerge.

The significance of the section in American history is that it is the faint image of a European nation and that we need to reëxamine our history in the light of this fact. Our politics and our society have been shaped by sectional complexity and interplay not unlike what goes on between European nations. The greater sections are the result of the joint influence of the geologists' physiographic provinces and the colonizing stocks that entered them. The result is found in popular speech in which New England, the Middle States, the South, the Middle West, etc., are as common names as Massachusetts or Wisconsin. The Census divisions are more definite and official designations. Of course, the boundary lines are not definite and fixed. Neither are those of European nations. These larger sections have taken their characteristic and peculiar attitudes in American civilization in general.

We have furnished to Europe the example of a continental federation of sections over an area equal to Europe itself, and by substituting discussion and concession and compromised legislation for force, we have shown the possibility of international political parties, international legislative bodies, and international peace. Our party system and our variety in regional geography have helped to preserve the American peace. By having our combination of sections represented in a national legislative body, by possessing what may be called a League of Sections, comparable to a League of Nations, if it included political parties and a legislative body, we have enabled these minority sections to defend their interests and yet avoid the use of force.

The thing to be avoided, if the lessons of history are followed, is the insistence upon the particular interests and ideals of the section in which we live, without sympathetic comprehension of the ideals, the interests, and the rights of other sections. We must shape our national action to the fact of a vast and varied Union of unlike sections.

Notes

1. *The Sea Base: Relation of Marine to National Transportation System and of Lakes to Ocean Route to Continental Traffic,* published by Great Lakes-St. Lawrence Tidewater Association (Duluth, Minn., 1923). For an argument in favor of the New York route, see John B. Baldwin, *Our Dardanelles* (Honolulu, 1924).

2. I have illustrated this subject in an article called "Sections and Nation," in the *Yale Review,* October, 1922.